The Fourth Power ✻

GARY HART

The Fourth Power

A Grand Strategy for the United States

in the Twenty-First Century ✴ ✴ ✴

2004

OXFORD
UNIVERSITY PRESS

Oxford   New York
Auckland   Bangkok   Buenos Aires   Cape Town   Chennai
Dar es Salaam   Delhi   Hong Kong   Istanbul   Karachi   Kolkata
Kuala Lumpur   Madrid   Melbourne   Mexico City   Mumbai   Nairobi
São Paulo   Shanghai   Taipei   Tokyo   Toronto

Copyright © 2004 by Oxford University Press, Inc.

Published by Oxford University Press, Inc.
198 Madison Avenue, New York, New York 10016

www.oup.com

Oxford is a registered trademark of Oxford University Press

Library of Congress Cataloging-in-Publication Data
Hart, Gary, 1936–
The fourth power : A grand strategy for the United States in the
21st century / by Gary Hart.
    p. cm.
ISBN 0-19-517683-9
1. United States—Foreign relations—2001– 2. National security—
United States. 3. United States—Military policy. 4. United States—
Politics and government—2001. 5. World politics—1989– I. Title.
E895.H37 2004
327.73′009′0511—dc22   2004001444

9 8 7 6 5 4 3 2

Printed in the United States of America
on acid-free paper

A good cause is a sword as well as armour.

. . . while the horizon of strategy is bounded by the war, grand strategy looks beyond the war to the subsequent peace. It should not only combine the various instruments [financial, diplomatic, and ethical], but so regulate their use as to avoid damage to the future state of peace—for its security and prosperity. The sorry state of peace . . . that has followed most wars can be traced to the fact that, unlike strategy, the realm of grand strategy is for the most part terra incognita—still awaiting exploration, and understanding.

—B. H. LIDDELL HART, *Strategy*

Preface ✳

The arguments put forward in this work are straightforward, if not simple. The early twenty-first century is characterized by revolutionary new realities. Following the end of the Cold War until the terrorist attacks of September 11, 2001, the United States lacked a national strategy for addressing these new realities and for applying its powers to its larger purposes. Beginning with the invasion of Iraq, that strategic vacuum has begun to be filled by a strategy of empire. An imperial strategy, however, violates the democratic republican principles upon which our nation is founded. Alternatively, a principled application of our economic, political, and military powers to the large purposes of providing security, enlarging opportunity, and expanding liberal democracy represents both a more comprehensive response to new revolutionary realities and a more plausible and effective grand strategy. Such a grand strategy can contribute to the restoration of the ideal of the American Republic.

A historic argument has been opened that the United States is, like it or not, an empire. The only issue, it is argued, is what kind of empire we will be. This is a false and dangerous proposition, one that misunderstands both the realities of our age and the authentic and unique character of America. Though the strategy of empire, especially as it has been demonstrated in Iraq and the Middle East, is refuted here, this work is not simply a polemic against the current U.S. administration. It is instead a positive effort to propose the framework for a national strategy to replace containment of communism while resisting both an ad hoc or reactive approach, on the one hand, and the theocratic approach to America's challenges, on the other hand. If the strategy proposed here were to be characterized, it would best be called the strategy of a principled republic.

It would be an act of presumption to suppose that any single individual could devise a grand strategy for the most powerful nation in human history. For this reason, this essay is meant to suggest why such a grand strategy is required, what the enterprise of strategy entails, some large purposes to which America's powers, underwritten by its principles, might be applied, and why the strategy of the American Republic is necessarily incompatible with empire, even benign empire.

In his historic essay in *Foreign Affairs* (1947), elaborating publicly on his previously private memorandum, George Kennan provided a central organizing principle—containment of communism—for America's role in the Cold War world. The complex twenty-first century, alas, has yet to yield itself to such a singular proposition. A war on terrorism will not serve. Even as it combats this new plague, the United States has too much else to do that is both positive and good.

The current essay knowingly risks criticism in at least two significant regards: it enters the policy realm enough to illustrate how certain large purposes might be achieved, and thus strays from classical strategic thought, but it does not go so far as to lay out a detailed blueprint sufficient to satisfy those searching for a programmatic vision of the future. Avoidance of this Scylla and Charybdis requires this work to be merely an "essay concerning . . ." that might stimulate the next George

Kennan, hopefully sooner rather than later. For mischief covets a strategic vacuum.

My preoccupation with a post–Cold War strategy dates to the early 1990s, as evidenced by my memorandum to President William Clinton, excerpted in the appendix.

To the degree this essay merits credit, it must be shared with a wide variety of friends, advisers, and associates, particularly former U.S. Senate staff members too numerous to mention, with whom I have worked in both public and private life. They are joined more recently by commissioners and staff of the U.S. Commission on National Security/21st Century, whose historic role in our nation's life is yet to be realized. And, not least, I wish to thank John Gaddis, Lovett Professor of History at Yale University; Paul Kennedy, Dilworth Professor of History at Yale; and Robert O'Neill, retired Chicele Professor of Military History at Oxford University for providing the groundwork for my modest knowledge of the nature and history of strategic thought.

Continuing thanks also go to my intelligent, insightful, and indefatigable editor, Dedi Felman, and Oxford University Press (USA).

GARY HART
Kittredge, Colorado

Contents ✳

The Fourth Power ✷

Introduction

G rand strategy has to do with the application of power and resources to achieve large national purposes. In the case of the United States in the twenty-first century, its powers are economic, political, and military. In each category these traditional powers are orders of magnitude greater than those of any other nation—friend or rival—and, in the case of military power, greater than those of most of the next several strongest nations combined. America also possesses a fourth power, the power of principle, which may well be one of its greatest strategic assets in the twenty-first century. Much depends on whether and how this asset is employed.

Today the United States possesses abundant, even historic, power. But we do not possess a grand strategy. We do not have a coherent framework for applying our powers to achieve large national purposes. There is not even a consensus as to what our national purposes are. We are much clearer about the sheer fact of our power than we are about how, when, where, and toward what ends it should be used.

There are general goods—peace, prosperity, and so forth—to which all Americans subscribe. But these are abstractions, and relative ones at that. Whose peace? How much prosperity?

Being for a "strong national defense" was such a political shib-boleth during the Cold War that it became a cliché. No one in favor of a weak defense was to be found.

The Cold War had the curious advantage of offering a large national purpose—containment of communism—and a simple, understandable one at that. It was a kind of central organizing principle around which political and military policies could be shaped, resources mustered, and the public engaged. For the period between 1946 and 1991, it became a simplified form of grand strategy for the United States and many of its allies.

Strategically all was well until the virtually overnight collapse of the Soviet Union and, with it, the threat of com-munist expansion against which containment was arrayed. Suddenly—in late 1991—containment of communism as a strategic focus lost its relevance. The United States, suddenly the world's sole superpower, found itself triumphant but stra-tegically adrift. Overnight it lost its largest, single national purpose, any coherent notion of its principal goals, and any sense of how to apply its economic, political, and military power to achieve them.

During the last decade of the twentieth century, it was not as if the triumph of democracy—the "end of history" it was called—brought with it a utopian golden age. Trouble, some of it repressed during the bipolar ideological struggle of the second half of the twentieth century, abounded. Artificial states, such as Yugoslavia, collapsed in turmoil. African tribes slaughtered each other with machetes, and warlords chased the world's greatest power from Somalia. Drug cartels under-took to control Colombia. New mafias arose out of the politi-cal rubble of the former Soviet Union. An epidemic of new conflicts fathered by ancient grievances stimulated nostalgia for the strategic simplicity of the Cold War. A decade marked by confusion and sporadic local conflict transpired.

Then came September 11, 2001. Nineteen suicidal young men armed with tradesmen's tools converted four commercial aircraft into guided missiles and killed 3,000 Americans. At the least, this event signaled the resumption of history, albeit in a new and complex form. But, unlike communism's perceived threat to Europe, Asia, Africa, and Latin America, this event failed to provide a new central organizing principle equivalent to containment of communism.

For the time being, the "war on terrorism," with its overthrow of the governments of Afghanistan and Iraq, has sufficed to fill the vacuum of national purpose. For our current administration it offers a guiding principle for the moment, a principle it did not previously possess. But few would argue that this war *by itself* represents an American grand strategy— the application of its powers to large national purposes—worthy of a great nation. Rather, terrorism and the responses it requires might best be seen as a metaphor for an emerging new revolutionary age to which a national grand strategy must respond.

The first step in erecting the framework for such a new grand strategy requires an understanding of the historical realities that characterize our age. In contrast to the relatively static and linear twentieth-century Cold War, the early twenty-first century is multidimensionally revolutionary. Globalization, the name given the internationalization of commerce and finance, is fundamentally transforming markets and challenging the authority of central banks and national sovereignty over financial and regulatory structures. Capital flows and multinational corporate entities negotiating complex cross-border transactions are defying national constraints.

Simultaneously, the information revolution, the historical equivalent of the Industrial Revolution of the early nineteenth century, is transforming the economies of the advanced world and expanding the divide, in this case a so-called digital divide, between the developed and the underdeveloped worlds. The advent of the silicon chip and microminiature processors has transformed productivity, revolutionized the workplace, and explosively expanded communications—at least for those on the positive side of the digital divide.

These two economic revolutions have contributed to the eroding authority of the nation-state, the fundamental political building block since the mid–seventeenth century. Not only have national financial regulatory structures suffered from the internationalization of commerce, but tribalism, fundamentalism, privatization, and other forces of disintegration have begun to seriously challenge the authority of the state and its ability to guarantee social and economic stability. Added to that, nonstate actors, especially terrorist organizations but also tribes, clans, and gangs, challenge the state's monopoly on violence and its compact with its nation's citizens to provide security in exchange for loyalty.

This phenomenon, terrorism, represents a final twenty-first-century revolution, the transformation of the nature of conflict. States no longer control when, where, and how violence—war—will be conducted and whether it will be organized and carried out in accordance with established international conventions. Instead, terrorism and its antecedents, mafias, cartels, tribes, clans, and gangs, owe allegiance to no state, often have no political objectives, and directly target civil society.

Thus, globalization, the information revolution, eroding nation-state authority, and the changing nature of conflict are the twenty-first-century realities upon which and in response to which the framework for an American grand strategy must be constructed. To neglect these new revolutionary realities, to assume the new century will be merely a linear extension of the last, is an invitation to folly and failure.

A further and equally dangerous error is to assume that, because of its unrivaled power, the United States is at liberty to do as it wishes, that it can flaunt its power, bully its inferiors, and unilaterally exercise its own will. One of the unavoidable realities of America's jarring entry into the twenty-first-century world, and one of that entry's historic ironies, is that we are both envied and resented. Much of the envy is based on the great disparity in standard of living between the United States and the less developed world, which is to say much of the rest of the world. Some, though by no means all, of the resentment is inarticulate, and some is hypocritical. Nonetheless, both envy and resentment are real, and they are fed by policies and behavior that are imperious, unilateral, insensitive, and arrogant. Therefore, in addition to recognizing the revolutionary realities of the twenty-first century, the United States' new grand strategy must also recognize our nation's constraints, constraints resulting from our citizenship in the world community, our lifestyle and patterns of resource consumption, the transparency of our actions through global access to instant information, and genuine concerns about America's behavior, practice, and exercise of its powers.

More explicitly, the United States is a member, and usually the leading member, of a number of twentieth-century bilateral and multilateral organizations and alliances. The North Atlantic Treaty Organization (NATO) is the most prominent of these, but dozens of others bind the United States, so long as it agrees to be bound, to certain cooperative commitments. In the early years of the new century, the U.S. government either directly challenged many of these commitments or assumed it was at liberty to act as it wished regardless of their terms. Strategic planning requires that those obligations and commitments be either acknowledged and taken into account or formally abrogated, with acceptance of all the consequences attendant thereto, rather than being selectively observed when it seems convenient to do so. Our willingness to adopt a unilateralist course at the turn of the new century prompted one senior foreign policy expert to conclude, "American power worldwide is at its historic zenith. American global political standing is at its nadir."[1] In an interdependent world, the sheer fact of power is less important than the way it is employed.

An additional constraint on strategy is America's continued dependence on foreign natural resources, especially petroleum supplies to fuel its increasing energy demands. A coherent national strategy needs to acknowledge and take into account this dependence, either to fully support it militarily or to reduce it. A twenty-first-century grand strategy is obliged to deal seriously with this dependence so central to America's way of life.

Further, the United States is constrained by its increasing demand for foreign investment to finance its debt and even to pay for its defenses. This constraint is most graphically illustrated by America's huge trade, or balance of payments, deficits and by its reliance on foreign public and private investors in the amount of $500 billion or more each year. Like other constraints, the economic and security implications of this dependence must be taken into account as the search for a new national strategy is pursued.

Finally, though by no means exhaustively, America is (or at least ought to be) constrained by its own constitutional heritage, its espoused beliefs and ideals—in short, its principles as a republic. The exigencies of the Cold War led the United

States to erode and sometimes violate those principles in its perceived need to protect itself. The historic antecedents for abandonment of its highest principles were often characterized as realpolitik or justified as *raison d'etat*. Of all the constraints under which the United States operates in the new twenty-first century and which most require attention in devising a grand strategy, American adherence to its own principles offers the most compelling challenge. This is particularly true if one accepts the premise offered here that America's fourth power, its principles, represents one of its most potent assets, and if one accepts the further premise that the exercise of this fourth power, the power of principle, inevitably conditions the ways in which the three traditional powers of economics, politics, and the military are exercised.

Strategy would, arguably, be simpler if it were played out on the horizontal plane (as many suppose it to be) of the use of power, particularly military power, to deter or respond to threats, to achieve dominance, or to obtain national objectives such as securing supplies of oil. But America's larger purposes must embrace opportunities as well as threats, possibilities as well as constraints, and progress as well as decay. In short, large national purposes and the resources applied to achieve them must include clear-eyed, practical, and realistic ways of alleviating the human condition both for its own sake as a humanitarian ideal and as a strategy to reduce the conditions and causes of violence and the widespread resentment of American wealth. People with authentic hope for a better life seldom seek out the terrorist's camp.

Twenty-first-century strategists will see economic and political power as of equal importance to military power and, in some instances, of even more effective influence. A threat never born is a victory won. If a standard principle of military strategy is the concentration of maximum force at the decisive point of impact, the same must be true of economic development, financial investment, diplomatic attention, and benign political influence. Thus, twenty-first-century grand strategy becomes a multidimensional chessboard much more than a war game table, a relief map of peaks, contours, and depressions rather than a flat surface. And the powers and resources brought to bear on the objective represent assets that change with circumstances—today a pawn, tomorrow a knight. On one occasion U.S. Special Forces point laser designators at distant mountain caves to direct precision-guided ordinance to the target. On another occasion humanitarian relief workers feed starving refugee children. On one occasion cruise missiles fired from unmanned aircraft destroy a chemical weapons arsenal. On another occasion wells are drilled and irrigation systems built to grow food for drought-stricken villagers. A serious strategist will appreciate the importance of both approaches, indeed, of a multitude of approaches, some never before conceived, to the advancement of America's purposes.

These examples illustrate yet another characteristic of strategy, the distinction between means and ends. It would be especially troublesome, and potentially even dangerous, for the "war on terrorism" to be mistaken for a national strategy. If the purpose is to defeat terrorism, means other than or in addition to force must be employed. This is especially true in a new century whose revolutionary realities do not lend themselves to purely one-dimensional military response.

This is even more true of the recently redefined doctrine of preemption, as a self-proclaimed right to initiate a military attack on a nation or set of actors perceived to represent a *potential,* but not imminent, threat—what President George W. Bush has called a "sufficient threat." Leaving aside complex and troublesome questions of national morality and international law, to elevate a doctrine such as preemption to the level of strategy, let alone grand strategy, is seriously to misunderstand the strategic enterprise.

Preemption in this preventive context is little better than an organic impulse—I'll strike you before you strike me. Such an impulse, or doctrine if you wish, falls far short of grand strategy. To declare a policy of anticipatory self-defense or preventive war may, at best, be seen as one doctrinal facet of a greater military strategy. But, even so, it is but one of a large number of options open to policy makers and military commanders to carry out much larger objectives contained in the serious grand strategy of a major power. And if preemption is exercised at the expense of alliance, as in Iraq, the result may well be less, rather than more, security.

Likewise, much the same could be said of notions such as containment. Containment in the Cold War context might rise to the level of national strategy, in that its historic context was an epic struggle involving one great block of nations resisting a perceived hegemon represented by a distinctly aggressive ideology and another great block of nations. Containment of terrorism as a strategic concept, however, falls far short of the strategic objective of a great power applying national resources to achieve large purposes.

In this new revolutionary age America's large purposes may include, but must be much greater than, containment or even elimination of terrorism. Terrorism is both an immediate threat and a symptom of greater challenges, including widespread resentment of American power, foreign policy, and commercial culture. They include threats to increasingly fragile oil supplies. They include intricate and complex international financial systems vulnerable both to cyber attack and to the domino effect of global recession. They include failed and failing states and the challenge of forces of disintegration, such as tribalism, to traditional nation-states.

These are examples of a much larger phenomenon, the revolutionary world of the twenty-first century, a world requiring not only new approaches but also a new mentality that appreciates the interrelationship of these new challenges and the interrelationship of the necessary and appropriate responses to them. This is the response to those who might ask, Why the need for a grand strategy?

Grand strategy, in the classic sense used here, is a systematic, ordered, coherent enterprise that takes into account our nation's total resources, its capabilities and constraints, and its traditions, culture, and values to achieve great objectives that include, but are not limited to, its own security. At least to the degree that the two political parties represent consensus thinking in America and the political potential to implement that thinking, the two "strategic" options they have produced for consideration are the reactive approach and the theological approach.[2]

During the unstructured, post–Cold War 1990s, the president's national security adviser was heard to disclaim any notion of an overarching strategy and to advocate an ad hoc approach to the crises that might (and did) arise. This reactive approach certainly is an alternative to grand strategy. The current government's theological approach to security issues—the "axis of evil"—is, of course, another. Arguably, both qualify as "strategy" in the most prosaic sense of the word.

Before George W. Bush cloaked this prestrategy point of view in theological terms, however, it was taking shape in the minds of some who were to become his advisers. Scarcely had the Cold War grown permanently cold and the armies of Saddam Hussein, such as they were, been driven back to Baghdad in 1991 than the idea of America as empire took root and began to be discussed in narrow ("neoconservative") circles.

In terms of official foreign policy, this imperial ambition went nowhere, that is, until the terrorist attacks of September 2001. Then an invasion to root out al Qaeda networks in Afghanistan became the centerpiece of the war on terrorism. Once the ruling Taliban was overthrown in Afghanistan and al Qaeda leadership driven underground, the question then became, What next? Newly clad in their theological garments, the advocates of empire marched on Baghdad.

Now in the brief time since terrorism came to America, a literature of America-as-empire has sprung up. Though at present it is surreptitious, the notion of an imperial strategy wafts its way through Georgetown salons and neoconservative policy centers. The general idea seems to be (and it must for now be "seems," since no one in an official position has come right out and said it) that the post–Cold War world requires a benign hegemon and superpower organizer, otherwise vicious forces such as terrorism will erupt, and Providence has presented the United States with this mission.

Two problems arise with this neo-imperial strategy, both requiring considerable attention: the American people do not see their nation as an empire; and the ultimate price of empire is the sacrifice of the American Republic.

This essay challenges these two current approaches—the reactive and the theological—on two grounds: they are inadequate as coherent guides for American action required to address the new realities of the twenty-first century; and they are not strategies in any meaningful sense of the word. More traditional strategies of containment, unilateralism, hegemony, and isolationism must also be analyzed for their potential relevance to twenty-first-century realities. In each case, however, the four revolutions of globalization, information, sovereignty, and conflict challenge their relevance. Additionally, a vision of empire, especially a theocratic one, directly challenges America's status as a republic.

A new grand strategy for the United States in the twenty-first century should assume the following characteristics: it will be multidimensional; it will transcend impulse, reaction, and ideology; it will rely on appropriate means to achieve justifiable ends; it will recognize its own constraints; and it will be transparent. But it must also acquire at least three other characteristics. The new grand strategy must be consistent. It cannot erect a doctrine such as preemption as a centerpiece of policy and then apply that doctrine only to weak states easily conquerable. It must be coherent; its various elements must relate to each other in operation and execution. And it must be adaptable. Cold War deterrence began to fray and lose relevance as the Soviet Union began to redefine itself in the late 1980s. Times change, and methods and means also must change. Only principles remain constant.

By definition, to be meaningful a grand strategy must be relevant, and relevance must be gauged by the strategy's applicability to the realities it must address. The test is not coherence in the abstract but implementation in the context of the concrete realities of the times.

A grand strategy centered around the fourth power of national principle and the application of the other three powers—economics, politics, and the military—based on national principle must directly address the revolutions of globalization, information, sovereignty, and conflict; thus, they will be discussed with some specificity in that context. Structurally, then, this essay will first examine the revolutionary realities of the times. In what kind of world do we now live, and is it sufficiently new and different to require new strategic thinking? Then, the United States' powers, resources, and assets will be assessed. Some attention will be given to strengths and assets not conventionally called upon. What are the national strengths available to us? Next, constraints on the United States' exercise of its powers and employment of its resources will be more fully analyzed. What are the genuine limits on our powers? Thereafter, traditional strategies and policies that now pass for strategies will be critiqued for their relevance to new twenty-first-century realities. Important terms such as "security" and "preemption" must be defined with some precision. Is current thinking adequate to new twenty-first-century realities, and does it take adequate account of both our strengths and our limitations? Finally, on the basis of this foundation, considerable attention must then be paid to America's goals and purposes. What are America's definable goals in the new century, and what priority do we give to them?

Answers to these questions will help provide the framework for a grand strategy for the United States in the early twenty-first century. I will then seek to propose the United States' large national purposes and how we should apply our powers to achieve these large national goals.

Our nation's large purposes are to provide security, to expand opportunity, and to promote liberal democracy. A proper understanding of security in this revolutionary age will require application of all three powers—economic and political, as well as military—to achieve it. Before the United States can expand opportunity for others, it must increase and further expand opportunity at home. This will require political will and economic imagination. Expanded opportunity at home both increases security and creates the resources required to strengthen America's economic, political, and military powers, so that all three of these traditional powers can be employed to promote expanded opportunity, security, and liberal democracy abroad. America's large purposes are inter-related, and each requires the application, in varying degrees, of all our powers to achieve them.

More attention must be paid to these large purposes and the detailed application of our powers to achieve them. Before doing so, however, it will be necessary to consider the nature of the strategic enterprise. What is the nature of our powers and our resources available to that enterprise? Under what limits and constraints do we operate? How do our principles both empower and restrain us? What barriers do we face in framing a grand strategy? And why should our principles be brought to bear in our strategy at all?

Finally, after considering how to apply our powers to achieve our purposes, to define our unique role in the world, we must consider who we are—are we an empire or a republic? This has become our most critical choice at this moment in our history. If we are to remain a republic, as I strongly argue we must, then we must take definite steps to resist the temptations of empire and to restore our republican ideals and principles.

I ✳

Strategy in an Age of Revolution

It matters a great deal to the strategic project whether the times are quiescent or turbulent. Terrorism, failed states, and market gyrations have already made the early twenty-first century turbulent, and more surprises await. Two massive and historic economic revolutions, globalization and information, are simultaneously opening new markets, breaking down trade and regulatory barriers, and creating new opportunities. And they are, especially in the case of the information revolution, altering social life as well. But these revolutions are also further dividing haves from have-nots. Societies that have resources, finished products, or services to trade and those with widespread access to information technologies are benefiting substantially from these revolutions. Those with little to trade, and with little access to information technologies (the downside of the "digital divide"), are being left further behind to struggle against mounting tides of instability and disintegration.

As these economic and social revolutions elevate some parts of the globe and depress others, they are having profound political consequences as well. In addition to expanding gaps between haves and have-nots, including within the domestic structures of advanced economies, they are eroding the sovereignty and authority of the nation-state. Some three and a half centuries ago, states (or governments) struck bargains with nations (or peoples) whereby the state offered a degree of economic stability and collective security in exchange for the loyalty of the nation.

Such bargains held so long as governments could fulfill their side of the agreement. But globalization, or the internationalization of finance, commerce, and business, is eroding the ability of state instruments—central banks, finance ministries, and treasury departments—to regulate national economies. Early twenty-first-century America has seen the weakening of traditional monetary policies, in the form of expansion and contraction of money supplies, and of traditional Keynesian fiscal policies, in the form of tax cuts and increased government spending. For almost two years, neither proved effective at countering persistent economic stagnation. The Federal Reserve Board lowered interest rates at least eleven times—and, for many months, there was little economic response. The federal government provided massive tax cuts (thus ensuring massive budget deficits)—and consumer confidence was stagnant. The internationalization of financial markets makes traditional national fiscal and monetary policies increasingly suspect. Over time this inability to ensure economic promise and livelihood erodes the confidence of the people in their government.

Similarly, terrorist attacks signal the inability of the state to guarantee personal security, as well as security of the home, the community, and the homeland. The short-term response to terrorism was national unity. The longer-term response, if terrorist attacks continue, will be erosion of people's confidence in their government and its ability to protect them. Thus, if traditional economic solutions become decreasingly effective and if new forms of conflict threaten elementary security expectations of citizens, the sovereignty of the state is eventually called into question.

The final revolution, the transformation of war, becomes a central factor in strategy. Traditionally wars have been fought by uniformed armies in the field, exchanging men and matériel, until one side concedes and the other triumphs. Rules of war, including in international law and the Geneva conventions, eventually came to protect prisoners of war, civilians, and noncombatants and to guarantee justice against war criminals deemed to have violated these international legal mandates.

The new age of terrorism signals a dramatic departure from "civilized" warfare. Suicidal attackers wearing no uniform employ nonmilitary means to slaughter civilians, noncombatants, and nonmilitary targets. They have no political agenda other than to create maximum casualties, property damage, and fear. Such forms of conflict challenge traditional military assumptions, such as that threats of violence are mounted by other nation-states, conventional (and sometimes strategic) assets are the best defense against such attacks, increasingly sophisticated weapons systems will deter and respond to such threats, and superior numbers in force structures and weapons guarantee security. Further, in the case of the United States, benign North American neighbors and wide oceans historically represented our most important strategic assets and protection. All such familiar assumptions are now called into question.

Now a new concept—"homeland security"—has entered the national vocabulary. It has already required the largest reorganization of national government in a half century, produced heightened domestic threat warnings, established limited inoculation efforts, created household emergency stockpiling programs, and forced Americans to look over their shoulders, not a familiar activity. Overnight the new century looked substantially different from a more dependable twentieth century, where the threat was singular and where, with rare exceptions such as the Cuban missile crisis, the danger was remote. All has changed. The transformation of war is now a central strategic reality.

Thus, globalization and information are revolutionizing economies and societies. These revolutions are, in turn, weakening nation-state authority. The revolution in warfare—to the degree it erodes citizen confidence in government security guarantees—further threatens to contribute to the erosion of state sovereignty. History will treat our era—featuring these multiple transformations—as one of the most revolutionary in the modern age.

All of which argues for revolutionary, nontraditional thinking to underpin a new grand strategy. Indeed, to think traditionally in a revolutionary age is to guarantee the irrelevance of any strategy that thinking may produce. Thus the U.S. Commission on National Security/21st Century offered this prediction as early as September 1999:

> While the likelihood of major conflicts between powerful states will decrease, conflict itself will likely increase. The world that lies in store for us over the next 25 years will surely challenge our received wisdom about how to protect American interests and advance American values. In such an environment the United States needs a sure understanding of its objectives, and a coherent strategy to deal with both the dangers and the opportunities ahead.[1]

Strategy and Grand Strategy

Perhaps one of the reasons politicians and political thinkers resist the notion of strategy in any structured sense is its overly narrow identification with war. If blame is due for this, it must begin with Carl von Clausewitz, the father of modern strategy, in whose classic *On War* this definition is provided: "Strategy [is] the use of engagement for the object of the war." And, of course, war was simply the pursuit of policy by other means. A current Clausewitzian, Colin Gray, defines strategy as "the use that is made of force and the threat of force for the ends of policy."[2]

Even the father of the "indirect approach" in strategy (following Sun Tzu), B. H. Liddell Hart, restricts strategy narrowly: "the art of distributing and applying military means to fulfill the ends of policy."[3] On the broader subject of grand strategy Hart acknowledges that "fighting power is but one of the instruments of grand strategy—which should take account of and apply the power of financial pressure [economics], of diplomatic pressure [politics], of commercial pressure, and, not least of ethical pressure [principle], to weaken the opponent's will." Even within the context of grand strategy, however, he places emphasis on pressure on an opponent, rather than on seeking ways to use these powers to avoid conflict and confrontation.

Edward Mead Earle assumes Liddell Hart's multidimensional understanding of grand strategy: "The highest type of strategy—sometimes called grand strategy—is that which so integrates the policies and armaments of the nation that the resort to war is either rendered unnecessary or is undertaken with the maximum chance of victory."[4] But, once again, the shadow of warfare cast by Clausewitz darkens and limits the definition of grand strategy.

It is left to the historian Paul Kennedy to provide the basis for the broad understanding of grand strategy employed here. The student of grand strategy, he asserts, must take into account a large number of factors not included by military historians, including "the critical importance of husbanding and managing national resources," "the vital role of diplomacy . . . in gaining allies, winning the support of neutrals, and reducing the number of one's enemies," and "the issue of national morale and political culture."[5] These are somewhat different ways of suggesting my large purposes of achieving security, creating opportunity, and promoting liberal democracy, all within the bounds of national principle.

Powers, Resources, Assets, and Strengths

At the point where America's large purposes are defined, it will then be important to know the powers available to achieve those purposes. In a word, the United States is the world's strongest economy. Its economic output represents almost a third of the total world's output and is greater than that of the next four largest economies combined. It is the most powerful political presence on earth. We have an unrivaled diplomatic network administering scores of treaties, alliances, and bilateral relationships. And, within a decade, our nation will spend more on its military power every year than the entire remainder of the world collectively. Given its overwhelming superiority in the three traditional powers—economic, political, and military—it would seem simple to conclude that the United States can do whatever it wishes. It can achieve any large purpose it may devise. Its unrivaled strengths make it a colossus astride the globe.

Were all this true, it would make the strategic enterprise a simple one. Alas, twenty-first-century reality is not so simple. Many assets, traditionally perceived to be strengths, turn out to be liabilities; many assets are empowering only if correctly utilized. According to one school of thought, political nature abhors an unrivaled power, and therefore a power to counterbalance the United States will eventually emerge, probably sooner rather than later. Some believe that power could be a united Europe. Others hold that it will be China. Still others believe Europe will represent the countervailing economic power and China will become a military rival. And still others expect a rival or alliance of rivals that is impossible to identify today.

On the other hand, according to Samuel Huntington's thesis, post–Cold War rivalry will be less between and among individual nation-states and more between and among cultures and civilizations.[6] To the degree this view reflects reality, and current evidence of confrontation between the United States and much of the Arab and Islamic worlds suggests this might be at least partially true, the resources of a single nation, even the most powerful one, matter less than the combined resources of the nation's allies in a common Western civilization challenged by a competing civilization or culture.

Two observations are required. First, the "Western" world is badly divided in its approach to Islam. Much of Western Europe, Canada, and Latin America does not see itself as threatened by or in conflict with Islam or its Arab component. Therefore, it is difficult to see a united post-Enlightenment Western world in confrontation with the Arab Middle East or the wider Islamic world. Second, Islamic emigration into much of Europe is obscuring that continent's singular character as a Judeo-Christian, Western product of the Enlightenment era. And, to a lesser degree, Latin American emigration into the United States—which has increased to more than 35 million the number of people from Spanish-speaking countries—is altering the historical economic and political hegemony of Anglo-Saxon/European elements in America.[7] Thus, massive shifts in emigration and multiculturalism are challenging the notion of unitary civilizations and their capability or willingness to act in harmony, especially in opposition to other civilizations.

Nevertheless, the United States' economic and military superiority gives it strategic leverage currently unmatched either by a single power or by any current power collective. Reality also dictates, however, that unilateral exercise of power, for example, through protectionist or mercantilist economic policies, while effective at least temporarily in enriching oneself and disadvantaging others, will also be self-defeating over the longer term in an increasingly integrated world. This phenomenon will be further analyzed in the discussion of constraints on the exercise of power.

Traditionally overlooked in strategic thinking are intangible powers, resources beyond normal economic and military assets. A great deal of attention has been paid to the attraction of the American lifestyle, our commercial choices, our comforts, our economic opportunities. It is but a short distance between admiration and envy and then between envy and resentment, however; this is particularly true when disproportionate consumption of resources, in contrast with much of the rest of the world, is required to maintain our expansive (and expensive) way of life. American strategy must sift those qualities that make us distinctive (and attractive), for example, liberality, generosity, and diversity, from those that engender resentment, such as profligacy, arrogance, and bellicosity.

Of even greater strategic importance are America's principles, our freedoms but also our highest ideals, our standards, our noblest beliefs. These principles are subversive of older, hierarchical, class- and tradition-driven societies. They are also enormously appealing to those, especially the young, who can envision more freedom, a better way of life, and a more open social order.

Limits and Constraints

As appealing as it may be to some to believe the United States is now at liberty to do as it pleases and to dictate terms to the rest of the world, things are not so simple. As world leaders we are, at least to some degree, accountable for our behavior to our own people and to the peoples of other nations. We hold ourselves to a high standard and, therefore, are held by others to that same, or an even higher, standard.

One of the constraints under which we operate is transparency. Very little that our government does goes unnoticed in the world. Pursuing a policy carried over from the Cold War that "the enemy of our enemy is our friend" inevitably results in disclosure and condemnation when questionable, and sometimes outright despicable, alliances are disclosed. Those for whom power, especially in its military form, is the defining factor of strategy will exhibit little concern for disclosure of questionable or unprincipled behavior. But for most Americans, who take their ideals seriously, their government should stand for something nobler than expediency. Thus, at home and abroad, transparency of national action becomes a constraint for a power that prides itself on its values.

In the past we have also been constrained by our alliances, such as the North Atlantic Treaty Organization (NATO), and the willingness of our allies to cooperate with or at least endorse American military or political action. And we have, at least to some degree, attempted to coordinate monetary policies through such organizations as the G-8 and multilateral lending through the World Bank and the International Monetary Fund. The United States also participates in a variety of regional multilateral institutions, such as the Asian Development Bank, and is a signatory to hundreds of bilateral and international treaties. In short, we are bound legally and politically, by duty, and even by moral constraint by a wide range of commitments solemnly undertaken.

Despite all this we are, of course, capable of acting unilaterally (amply demonstrated by early Bush administration actions) or with nominal coalitions ("coalition forces," as our government chooses to call them) as in the Iraq war or larger coalitions of the willing as in Gulf War I. As in Iraq, our leaders are at liberty to decide to act virtually alone and even in direct contradiction or opposition to our allies' wishes. But in each case there is some price to be paid in international goodwill, future cooperation, and strategic dependability. We have already found it difficult to brush aside China's and Russia's opposition to our invasion of Iraq and then seek their intervention on our behalf against a greater threat in North Korea. A great power cannot permit the use of its powers to be defined by others. It must, however, calculate the price of damaged alliances in weighing the costs and benefits of unilateral action contrary to alliance commitments or international support.

As a dominant net energy consumer, one dependent for half its petroleum consumption on offshore sources, the United States is constrained in the use of its powers.[8] Politically it must seek favor with oil-producing nations and regions. Its foreign policies, its diplomacy, and its willingness to court the goodwill of politically incompatible regimes are all affected by such large-scale energy dependence. Looked at in another way, were the United States miraculously to be free of oil dependence, one can imagine how different our policies in the wider Persian Gulf region, for example, might be. Gulf War I was unquestionably fought to liberate Kuwait's oil from Iraqi control. And, at the very least, oil played *some* role in the Iraq war fought a decade later.

Our European allies and Japan, it is often argued, are even more dependent on Persian Gulf oil than we are. It is a great leap from this assertion to the conclusion that the United States is principally responsible for guaranteeing the oil supplies of the world, however. Since NATO is looking for a post–Cold War mission and purpose, the protection of worldwide petroleum production and distribution systems—including sea-lane straits and pipeline choke points—would be a natural task. In any case, dependence on oil is a major constraint on America's use of its powers and on its grand strategy for the twenty-first century.

The United States is also, on a massive scale, a debtor nation. Its needs to borrow from external lenders to finance its public debt are huge.[9] In addition, individuals also consume more than they earn, to the tune of $8.4 trillion in 2003, and finance the difference by short-term and long-term debt.[10] Our government's dependence on foreign investment represents yet another constraint on otherwise unconstrained exercise of its powers. Its fiscal and monetary policies, including whether we wish the dollar to rise or fall against other currencies, its trade policies, and a variety of other economic considerations all take into account our need for foreign loans. A weak dollar, for example, helps American exporters of goods and services compete in world markets but also weakens the incentive for foreign interests to purchase U.S. debt instruments.

As with energy dependence, debt dependence conditions a number of America's economic and political choices in ways that would not be the case if its current deficits were not so astronomical; in September 2003, the trade gap between the United States and the rest of the world had grown to $41.3 billion per month, or more than $500 billion annually.[11] One of America's most seasoned and respected financial experts, Ambassador Felix Rohatyn, summarized the constraints on a debtor nation as follows:

> To service our foreign debt of $3 trillion requires an inflow from abroad of $1.5 billion daily. Our answer has been to encourage a global devaluation of the dollar; this may help our exports for some time but also has negative effects. It is obvious that deliberately devaluing the dollar is not a policy that is likely to encourage foreign investment in the United States. Asian central banks now own almost $700 billion in U.S. Treasury bonds and have been financing our trade deficits and helping to sustain the value of the dollar. However, the 25 percent recent devaluation of the dollar implies an economic loss of almost $200 billion to the Asian central banks alone, a questionable incentive to maintain their American investments. We now run the risk of possible large increases in U.S. interest rates, and of a significant decline in the stock market if they were to slow their purchases. Keep in mind that foreigners own about $2 trillion or about 20 percent of all listed stocks in the United States.[12]

The Paradox of Principles

It is a paradox that America's greatest strength, its principles, may also be among its greatest constraints. A great deal of what maddens much of the world about the United States is another paradox: we oscillate between idealism and realism, between what we claim to believe about ourselves and how we actually behave in practice. We Americans are often blissfully unaware of how hypocritical we appear to other peoples when we act in contradiction to our stated values or when we refuse to acknowledge the obvious reasons for our behavior. Honest policies rarely are based on dishonest or even covert reasons.

For example: the world understood that oil played a great role in the decision to drive Iraq from Kuwait in 1991. Yet the first Bush administration twisted itself into a political pretzel in its attempt to avoid acknowledging this fact and to cloak our actions, rather, in the fiction of protecting "democracy" in Kuwait. For example: few outside the United States believed that the Iraqi government represented a terrorist threat to the United States, but that was the principal reason given for our invasion of Iraq in 2003. For example: we have paid much closer attention to political turmoil in Venezuela than to any other major South American nation because it has become a significant oil exporter. The subject of oil seems especially guaranteed to bring out the worst in us. And America's "interests" seem to lie disproportionately close to major oil reserves.[13]

An open society, and particularly one that prides itself on its openness as a feature of democracy, finds it awkward if not impossible to conceal its true purposes. As a democracy, the United States considers openness—or transparency of purpose and methods—one of our principles. We proclaim it and espouse it. Yet we are naïve to believe that we can conduct ourselves differently, that is to say secretly, on the world stage. Even more, when we do so, we become hypocritical. Only a sophisticated and cynical society, one practiced in deception and manipulation, and one small enough to conceal its secrets, can hope to offer one appearance and another behavior. If we are practicing to become an imperial power, we must abandon the principle of openness, at least, and probably a number of others.

Are we now, or are we in the process of becoming, an empire? Some argue we have been since 1898 and the Spanish-American War. Others say we have been since 1947 and the beginning of the Cold War. Still others claim we became an empire with the fall of the Soviet Union. And yet another group says the age of terrorism has given us little choice but to become an empire. The question to be addressed, if any of these claims is true, is what *kind* of empire?[14]

This, in fact, may represent the fundamental decision for the United States in the early twenty-first century. As the sole superpower, or some say "hyperpower," we are now confronting a historic crossroads concerning our role in the world. Adrift and unfocused until the first terrorist attacks in September 2001, the "war on terrorism," which surfaced doctrines of preemption and preventive wars, has become the catalyst for American action. As we are finding in Afghanistan and Iraq, however, preemption and "regime change"—or, stated more directly, government overthrow—inevitably require prevention of chaos and eventually prolonged nation-building in the aftermath of invasion. Nation-building requires continued occupation, a long-term military presence, interim administration (sometimes for a good deal of time), considerable financial and economic assistance, rebuilding infrastructures and providing social services, arbitrating among rival factions, and endless entanglement. All of these are hallmarks of even the most benign empires. And this is exactly where we now find ourselves in occupied Iraq.

To which the inevitable question arises: What principles of a democratic republic are sacrificed when it assumes the role of empire? The democratic republic of America is based on certain historical principles. These include, among other things, the constitutional liberties of its people; limited powers of government with its branches checked and balanced by a written Constitution; the rights of free speech, elections, press, and assembly; commitment to the rule of law; and freedom of religious belief. To these might be added transparency in international diplomatic dealings, reciprocity among nations, the universality of human rights, respect for the sovereignty of states, adherence to basic precepts of international law, and so forth.

Principles are violated or abandoned less in the abstract and more in their application. As with an individual, if the United States applies its power contrary to its principles, it risks its political, and eventually its moral, authority. Were it not for the distinctly idealistic nature of America's founding, this notion would seem absurd in a world of power politics. But America set itself apart at its founding. There is a distinctly exceptionalist pattern in the weave of the rhetoric and debate of the constitutional era. The very idea of a federated republic on a large scale was novel. The notion of a written Constitution defining and limiting the new government's powers was unique. The various devices built into the system permitting perpetual evolution were imaginative. Perhaps most important, the ideal of a nation founded on rights, ideals, and principles resonated most strongly among the founders, all immensely practical men.

Woodrow Wilson is widely regarded as having been a starry-eyed dreamer for imagining that some of America's principles might be exportable. Much of the post-9/11 Bush foreign policy rhetoric claims to be neo-Wilsonian and idealistic in its notion of democratizing the Arab world and exporting American values elsewhere. But Wilson's promotion of democracy was internationalist, not unilateralist, and was channeled through diplomacy, not introduced at the point of a bayonet. There is a vast difference between advocating, as I do, that America live up to its own principles and advocating, as the Bush administration does, that the rest of the world live up to America's principles. And there is an even greater anomaly in America's setting aside its own principles in the process of trying to force the rest of the world to live up to them.

The founders understood that "foreign entanglements" would inevitably require the United States to adopt traditional diplomatic practices they were trying desperately to rise above and separate themselves from. It was not that America was *better*; it was that America was *different*. It was, in a way, an ancient Christian dilemma: how to be *in* the world without being *of* the world.

The U.S. Commission on National Security/21st Century makes this point in a more secular fashion: "America must never forget that it stands for certain principles, most importantly freedom under the rule of law. . . . if America is to retain its leadership role, it must live up to its principles consistently, in its own conduct and in its relations with other nations."[15]

The constraint—and power—of principle will play heavily in the effort to devise a grand strategy for the United States in a new century that presents dramatically different threats and equally new opportunities.

Overcoming Barriers to Strategy

It is fantasy, one would suppose, to presume to be able to construct a coherent strategy for the world's greatest power, a mass democracy—and an increasingly diverse one—of almost 300 million people operating in the revolutionary world of a new century and new millennium. Better, the critic would say, to have "values" and perhaps a few definable goals at home and abroad, and to rely on those to respond to the unpredictable, even chaotic, events of these revolutionary times as the occasion requires. A "strategy" suggests a straitjacket, too inflexible to account for the myriad surprises of the day.

But "strategy" as used here is meant to be a coherent framework of purpose and direction in which random, and not so random, events can be interpreted, given meaning, and then responded to as required. Absent war, however, Americans have resisted "centralized planning" as socialistic, intrusive, and repressive of initiative and enterprise. Thus, one of the great challenges of strategic thinking in the current age is to convince Americans—and particularly those distrustful of their own government—that to have a national strategy is to *liberate* the nation's energies in purposeful ways rather than approach the world as representing "one damn thing after another" and as requiring only ad hoc responses.

Those who see the world through ideological lenses will particularly resist the strategic enterprise. What need for a coherent effort to apply power to purpose if one's worldview is simplified by elemental certainty? But, to construct a Manichean world of good and evil, where America's role is to eradicate evil, is to thrust the United States backward ten centuries to the age of the Crusaders and to presume a righteousness and purity we have yet to earn.

Instead, the new realities of the twenty-first century will yield themselves much less to ideological interpretation and confrontation than did those of the twentieth century and will require much more the anticipatory intelligence demanded by the enterprise of strategy. What if, as I believe, the doctrinaire orthodoxies of both left and right, liberal and conservative, have become so brittle and stale that they cannot respond to these new realities? Something must give when the world does not readily yield to one's static view of what it should be and how it should behave. Old truths do not fade; old systems of belief about what the truth is must inevitably do so.

Beyond ideology, conventional political thinking generally—across party lines—is a barrier. Since the loss of certainty and the convenient central organizing principle of "containment of communism" at the end of the Cold War, both American political parties have seemed content to operate on a freewheeling, but very dangerous, ad hoc plane. Neither party has shown interest in or any particular aptitude for strategic thinking. The strategic enterprise requires disciplined, conceptual thinking, not an attribute of late twentieth-century and early twenty-first-century American political life. It is easier indeed to take life's problems, whether terrorism, trade wars, or failed states, as they arise or, instead, to insist on a rigid set of ideologically orthodox shibboleths than to think ahead, apply forethought to anticipated scenarios, and have a plan for the proper application of one's powers. How else can one explain the almost demented ignorance (ignore-ance) by the U.S. national government of warnings of future terrorist attacks at the turn of this century?

The proposal offered here might be called "anticipatory democracy," not an approach America is familiar with but one that it will have no choice but to embrace. To anticipate, however, to look at, if not over, the horizon, requires casting off conventional thinking and acceptance of the strategic enterprise.

Since, from Sun Tzu forward, strategy has been traditionally defined in limited military terms, there will also be those who will resist enlarging the strategic enterprise from the battlefield to the broader "political" arena. Even a cursory reading of the classics of strategy, however, reveals a surprising applicability of the principles of the strategy of armed conflict to the multifaceted human endeavor, especially when that endeavor has to do with a great nation systematically applying its multiple powers to its definable larger purposes. I am aware of no ironclad prohibition against applying the best principles of strategy to the larger field of statecraft.

Neither rabid libertarianism, confirmed liberalism or conservatism, nor rigid militarism should represent an insurmountable obstacle to the notion that a major power standing at a complex intersection in a turbulent storm can thoughtfully and intelligently plot (as opposed to plod) its way forward toward a destination it determines to be in its highest and best interest. In its simplest terms, that is the strategic enterprise.

2 ✴

Our Principles as
an Element of Strategy

A merican democracy, as noted, is characterized by certain
principles embodied in our founding documents, especially the Constitution, and in our history and political culture. According to scholarly consensus, these principles were
largely the product of Enlightenment humanism, and they
represented the most advanced evolution in political thought.
A number of these principles are shared among all democracies, Western and otherwise, but some are more closely identified with the United States than with any other nation. Over
its almost 225-year life, America has applied its principles to
its foreign policy in any consistent manner only periodically.
Though many Americans choose to believe that we are unfail-
ingly faithful to our highest ideals, periodic cycles of principle
and pragmatism characterize our complex history. Therefore,
any account of America's principles, particularly one empha-
sizing principle as a component of strategy, must acknowledge
inconsistency and imperfection in application throughout our
nation's life.

We believe, above all else, in freedom, the principle by
which no one should suffer political oppression but everyone
should instead be at liberty to pursue his or her individual

destiny without interference from the state or from others. We believe that democracy is the best system to guarantee that freedom through its reliance on an open participatory process, political equality, and elected representation. The principle of meritocracy, the opportunity to achieve one's personal goals bounded only by one's talent, is central to American democracy. The supremacy of the rule of law, equal status under the law and protection by a just legal system, is a central American principle. Our principles embrace the sanctity of property and the protection of private property from intrusion and confiscation. We share with other nations an absolute belief in the right and necessity of protecting ourselves from attack. Finally, our principles dictate that we will resist (selectively, it must be admitted) oppression of others without seeking to oppress others ourselves.

More immediately and directly, we may state our principles in this form:

We have "unalienable rights" protected by a written Constitution from coercion by the state. Those rights are most clearly articulated in the Bill of Rights but are elaborated and expanded by judicial interpretation according to the changing realities of the age. The principle of individual rights protected by the rule of law is the single most attractive feature of the American constitutional order to economically and politically oppressed people around the globe. It possesses an almost mystical attraction to those longing for freedom and individual self-worth. The idea that government exists to protect, not oppress, the individual has an enormous power not fully understood by most Americans who take this principle for granted from birth. Far more nations will follow us because of the power of this ideal than the might of all our weapons.

We are entitled to vote for our representative leaders ("deriving their just powers from the consent of the governed"), and they are accountable to us for assuring our rights. The structures of political representation are established in the first and second articles of the Constitution, which provide for the removal from office of members of Congress and the president. Like the first principle of constitutional rights, representative government created by free and fair elections is an astounding concept to billions of people on the planet. In fact, even the most oppressed people understand that the two are inextricable; only a truly representative government, one fairly elected by all the people, can protect the individual. The powerful attraction of this ideal is the strongest argument possible for preventing corruption of our election systems.

We can achieve that which our talents permit us to without interference. Though not specifically a constitutional guarantee, implicit in our Constitution and laws is removal of artificial or political barriers to realization of our individual destinies. Or, as the Declaration of Independence states, we are entitled to "the pursuit of happiness." The pressure of immigrants to enter the United States is testimony to their understanding that, at least in theory and mostly in practice, our system sets limits only by individual talent and not by class or birth. In this respect, the "American dream," the notion of the absence of limits to achievement, is a principle more resonant abroad than at home, where it is largely taken for granted.

Additionally, a central purpose of the Constitution itself was to "ensure justice." Our laws do not provide special status for the wealthy and powerful over the poor and powerless (though financial good fortune offers clear advantage). Any question concerning "the equal protection of the laws" was removed by the adoption of the Fourteenth Amendment. As with America's other powerful principles, protection of the law and the right to a fair and impartial judiciary would be a miracle to the vast majority of the world's people. But, like individual rights, representation, and unlimited opportunity, our system of justice is a noble ideal in direct proportion to its continued integrity.

We also hold that our land and possessions cannot be taken from us by the state except under public necessity and even then not without just compensation. The Fifth Amendment provides due process of law protections of private property and the requirement of just compensation for property taken for public use. The principle of private ownership of property, protected (rather than threatened) by the state, has an immensely powerful attraction to most societies where such protections do not exist. Like other American principles, however, its power is eroded by the United States' identification with and support for regimes that do not recognize this principle.

We announce our intention to defend ourselves from attack against our citizens and nation. The Constitution was enacted, in part, to "provide for the common defense" and provides for "calling forth the militia . . . to repel invasions." Fundamental rights of individual and collective self-protection, however, require no further constitutional guarantees. The universal principle of the right of self-protection places great stress on the use of force only where danger is immediate and only when no other recourse is available. Resort to the practice of preemptive invasion and preventive war undermines our moral authority and our history as a benign power. What limited "respect" we engender by the questionable use of force is far outweighed by the price we pay for the sacrifice of the principle of self-defense.

We do not seek to dominate others and will resist those who seek to do so. Likewise, this principle arises more from the previous principles, as well as the character and history of the United States, than from any explicit constitutional provision. The unnecessary use of force is not limited to the military aspect. We may abuse our authority and status as a leading democratic power by coercive economic policies and arm-twisting diplomacy. All countries understand the concept of "national interest." But where the United States' national interest becomes an excuse for bullying and pressure, especially to achieve advantage for our private commercial interests, we stray from democratic leader to aggressive self-promoter. This is the very imperial precipice to which current policy has brought us, and it threatens to destroy the power of our ideals and principles.

Who in the world would not wish to live under a political system based on these and other such principles, principles of individual rights, representative government, rule of law, protection of private property, the benign exercise of power, and the ideal of nondomination? They represent the noblest ideals of human political aspiration. The power of these principles is sui generis, but it also rests in their inherent attractiveness to others not so blessed and in their consistent incorporation into American foreign policy. The difficulty is in their implementation, both at home and abroad, and in those occasions when they are not consistently followed.

Let us explore how these principles might be extended by application through our relations with the nations of the world.

Our commitment to freedom means that we will ally with free societies and oppose oppressive ones. Here danger lies. We supported oppressive regimes in Africa, Asia, and Latin America during the Cold War as an instrument of the containment of communism. The enemy of our enemy was our friend, however ruthless. In too many cases we sacrificed our principles for the perceived security such alliances might bring. We turned a blind eye to those regimes' suppression of opposition, in some cases democratic opposition. We permitted new leaders to be jailed, or killed, without objection. We are now in danger of committing the same sins, in states bordering Afghanistan, for example, in the name of combating terrorism.

That commitment to freedom means that we should encourage other nations to endorse liberty and adopt liberal democratic structures, systems, and processes. This is the alternative to becoming bedfellows with dictators in return for basing rights for our military or securing their supplies of oil for export to the United States.

Those nations and societies we favor and ally with should themselves be nations that seek to provide opportunity for all their people. This is our greatest challenge in the Islamic world where governments are not democratic, pluralistic, or liberal. Diplomatically, this challenge is to encourage by example and persuasive exhortation rather than dictation and demand. We have, at the same time, to secure their cooperation against terrorism and to shepherd them toward democracy.

Since we embrace the rule of law, we favor a world characterized by the rule of law. As twenty-first-century problems require international solutions, pressure will increase on the United States to honor agreements and expand international commitments rather than adopt our current unilateralist approach. We cannot encourage adherence to legal constraint while we are abrogating such constraints ourselves with Kyoto and the international judicial system.

Further, we will cooperate with all nations to promote and protect private property rights. This policy requires American corporations to be particularly scrupulous in their dealings with foreign partners and governments. If American companies are collaborating in projects that destroy or deny individual property rights, our principle of the sanctity of private property is mocked. The outreach of our private sector must not erode the principles of our public policy.

Our basic national sovereignty and our commitment to the common defense mean that we will permit no one to threaten or attack us with impunity. Two roads emerge, however. One road encompasses partnerships and alliances; the other represents shooting first and asking questions later. The first is represented by Afghanistan, the second by Iraq. The more complex the world becomes, the more attractive the ethics of the Lone Ranger. But the more security becomes a common good, the more the idea of the posse becomes necessary.

Finally, as a republic—in contrast with an empire—we will resist hegemony without seeking hegemony. We will ally with nations of goodwill to prevent any other power from exercising its dominion. But we will not seek dominion for ourselves. This notion must become the centerpiece of United States diplomacy and international relations. Coalitions are formed by roughly commensurate nations with equal purpose, not by token contributions from lesser nations to the designs of the dominant power. To talk of "coalition forces" in Iraq is a perversion of language. Empires seek hegemony in places such as the Middle East. Republics do not.

These principles for international relations are not so unrealistic as to be readily dismissed as impractical even in a cruel world. They may, however, be inconvenient in their application. And there is the point. In an age of realpolitik, imperial ambition, and power politics, principles become inconvenient. Convenience is only a narrow step from expediency. And nations, like individuals, cannot claim principle and behave expediently in violation of those principles. In the revolutionary information age, where deception finds little room to hide, this is even more true than when diplomacy was conducted largely in secret. Additionally, to adopt expediency in American foreign policy, that is to say, to abandon the standards Americans claim for themselves, as the easiest or quickest means to achieve a desired or favorable result almost always requires either deception of the American people or their willing acquiescence in unprincipled international conduct. Either way national pride (if not also national honor) is sacrificed and a price in national embarrassment is paid, and there are more significant costs than embarrassment and the loss of pride. The argument here is not strictly for principle over power in foreign policy. It is a more positive brief for incorporation of America's highest principles into the range of its powers, the more traditional military, economic, and political powers, applied to achieve an early twenty-first-century American strategy. Where some have seen American ideals as an inconvenience at best and an outright hindrance to the exertion of American power abroad at worst, America's core principles, its canon of beliefs, are a fourth power, a positive advantage, in achieving the nation's larger purposes in the new century.

Who we are gives us our strength. We start with natural advantages in the world given the desire of most of the world's peoples to share our norms, albeit in their own cultures where possible. They do not necessarily want to become us. They want to share what we have, what we have achieved, as much as possible under their own terms and conditions. They readily understand that our prosperity and material success are in large part the product of our political system, our political standards and beliefs. When we abandon our principles for short-term political or economic advantage, we abandon one of our greatest strengths. For America to act imperially, expediently, or ignobly is to weaken rather than strengthen itself. The principles outlined here, or any better version thereof, might become a national code of conduct, a compass, a set of reference points for the achievement of America's strategy in the twenty-first century.

So we must think, at all points and on all occasions, how to turn the natural appeal of our principles and beliefs to the achievement of our larger purposes. Rather than be seen as a hindrance to policy, our principles should be seen as among our greatest natural assets in today's world. And almost as a law of political nature, when we neglect, sidestep, or deny those principles—those ideals that define who we are—we weaken ourselves and lessen our chances of achieving larger national purposes.

Thus, the argument here is as much a pragmatic as an idealistic one. We have much greater chances of becoming who we should want to be, of uniting peoples of goodwill, of leading permanent coalitions of democratic societies, and of achieving a more just and perfect union if we adhere to our principles rather than evade them and deny that we have done so.

America is different, or at least we believe ourselves to be. America's authentic difference is in its ideals, beliefs, and principles, not in its materialistic achievements. Few, if any, other nations make the same claims for a more noble or principled approach to international interaction. But, as the United States has emerged as a dominant power, we have been increasingly faced with opportunities to exert our power that require us to choose between our principles, on the one hand, and what are perceived to be our "interests," on the other. Those "interests" often have to do with acquiring support in ideological struggles, protecting or acquiring access to resources such as oil, achieving regional "stability," protecting or promoting the interests of allies, or, in the age of terrorism, preempting those perceived to be potential threats. We have supported dictators and oligarchies, against principle, in each of these causes and in each of these causes left a message that when interest and principle seem to conflict, we will choose interest.

Policy based on interest has characterized national conduct throughout human history. There is nothing new in that. And on the best of occasions principle and interest coincide. We do what is right because it is in our interest to do so. But when policy based on interest collides with the notion of principled exceptionalism, the sense that we are a principled nation bound together by a set of noble ideals, hypocrisy—or, even worse, downright ignorance of this collision—surfaces. It is bliss for a great nation to believe itself to be exceptional and to behave exceptionally. It is confusion at best and cynicism at worst to claim one thing and do another. Here there may be a divide between America's leaders and the American people. If the American people believe that we act according to our principles when in fact we do not, then either we are deceived by our leaders or we have become willing participants in self-deception and attempted deception of others. In the former case this is why almost all dubious U.S. actions are accompanied by classified documents urging that the American public be kept in the dark.

Either way, where interest prevails at the expense of principle, the power of principle is sacrificed. The near-universal appeal of the principles underlying America's political system is undermined by our nation acting contrary to our claimed beliefs. If our historic principles are one of America's greatest strengths, the casual erosion of those principles by the expedient exercise of power weakens, rather than strengthens, our nation in the long term.

America's principles flow from the nature of the Republic—a democratic republic—created by the founders. Our form of government is inseparable from the principles on which it is based. America's democratic republican principles define it. To abandon, suspend, or evade those principles is to alter the very nature of the Republic. Therefore, America's principles are a power to be applied to its larger strategic purposes, but evasion of those principles erodes the power they represent and makes it harder rather than easier to meet our objectives. To preserve our core principles is to strengthen the American Republic, and to restore the Republic is to strengthen our ability to achieve our strategic objectives.

3 ✳

America's Large Purposes in the New Century

A merica's large purposes in the twenty-first century are to provide security for its people, to expand opportunity at home and abroad, and to promote liberal democracy in the world. Providing security is primarily a domestic concern, though it is inseparable from America's role in the world and therefore international security. Expanding opportunity is also principally a domestic purpose; but, in the age of globalization and information, it is likewise intertwined with expansion of opportunity worldwide. Promotion of liberal democracy is primarily a goal of America's international relations, and intimately linked with expansion of opportunity globally, but it must arise from the pursuit of a more perfect democracy at home.

Providing security in its broadest form will require the exercise of the economic, political, and military powers of the United States. Each of these powers will assume new forms. Globalization and the information revolution require new economic strategies. The changing nature of national sovereignty will require new political strategies. The transformation of warfare will require new military strategies, tactics, and doctrines, as well as new military capabilities.

Though "large," and therefore general in scope, each of these purposes—security, opportunity, and democracy—has multiple dimensions requiring specific strategies, policies, and programs for their realization. And in each case structuring these individual strategies will require choices. Great nations have many choices. Indeed, the array of choices a nation has is a measure of its powers. To have choices, to escape restraints, to possess maximum flexibility are measures of greatness.

But even the dominant power in the world still faces the question of *how* the array of choices should be ordered and whether, when, and how its powers should be exercised to achieve the selected choices and its larger purposes. Is it possible for a great power to define its large purposes, relate them to each other in a coherent way, and then apply its powers to their achievement? In other words, is it possible for a great power, the United States in this case, to develop a grand strategy? Conversely, are there consequences for *not* doing so?

The examples of great powers in history and the degree to which they did, or did not, have a grand strategy are of dubious applicability to the United States in the early twenty-first century, in that most great powers throughout history have been empires. Significantly, America now finds itself in a growing debate over whether it is an empire or a republic and, if it is in fact an empire, what kind of empire it should be. Regardless of the outcome of this debate, it would be a mistake to assume that the United States requires a grand strategy *only* if it aspires to imperial status or has had that status thrust upon it. This debate generally and the dangers of empire specifically deserve and receive separate attention.[1] For now, suffice it to say that we do not have to share the dreams of Rome to accept our great power status as a mighty republic and to require a coherent strategy for wielding our considerable powers in a new age. But the fact that we are a republic and not an empire also conditions the larger purposes we choose and how we apply our powers to achieve them. This is in part the reason that the constraints on our strategy and the exercise of our powers and the importance of our principles require considerable attention.

There are consequences, almost all of them unpleasant, for failure to think strategically. The alternative, dealing in an ad hoc fashion with challenges as they arise, invites—indeed, virtually guarantees—that consequential decisions about how, when, and where we exercise our powers will be made outside any coherent context. The consequences of this kind of "ad hoc-ery" are arbitrariness, inconsistency, confusion, and ultimately contradictory behavior. In the early twenty-first century this failure of coherent strategy has led us to preemptive war against Iraq and an uneven diplomatic approach to the much greater and more immediate threat represented by a nuclear-capable North Korea. Earlier we intervened, unsuccessfully, in tribal warfare in Somalia but not in the much more tragic tribal slaughter in Rwanda. We were internationalists during the Cold War and beyond; with the change of administration in 2001, we abruptly become unilateralist, without any coherent rationale for doing so. This is not the kind of steadfast predictability and dependability that gives comfort to one's allies and garners respect from one's adversaries. Nor is it characteristic of a great power.

This is not to say that America's national and international policies can be pre-programmed or machine tooled or that immediate, pragmatic responses are always to be shunned. Policy reflects contingency, and contingency simply means that reality is characterized by circumstance. And circumstance will dictate nuance, subtle and not-so-subtle adjustments and alterations in policy reflecting the reality of the moment. But over time a rapidly changing world will require us to rely on core principles to pursue well-established and long-term purposes employing appropriate powers if we hope not to confuse ourselves and confound our allies.

Are not the large purposes of any benign power always the same—to ensure peace and prosperity, to guarantee both the security and the economic livelihood of its people? Surely. But these goals must always be sought within, and adapted with specificity to, the historical context of the times. As every age exhibits some new features, some particular challenges, a major power's large purposes must be shaped by the realities that characterize its age. Isolation undoubtedly made sense at those moments in America's past when our relative weakness discouraged engagement. Unilateral action might be required where immediate threats—such as imminent and unavoidable attacks on the homeland—do not permit formation of coalition and consensus action. And even the nature of what constitutes "large" purposes may vary with the times. The Depression of the 1930s required massive government action to stabilize markets and create social safety nets. Periods of economic expansion require less dramatic measures to perpetuate prosperity. World wars require conscription and massive standing armies. Periods of relative peace do not.

The revolutionary economic and financial changes brought by globalization and the information age and the political changes in national sovereignty and the nature of conflict are central new realities. But other factors demand consideration. The quality of the environment is increasingly a public health concern that is both global and immediate and that suggests the emergence of a global common. Drought, famine, and disease are transnational in scope. Mass migration, from south to north, is now a major global social phenomenon altering the profile and complexion of northern societies. Energy production and distribution networks tie intricate webs of consumers with even more intricate webs of producers. In a word, the early twenty-first century is a period of revolutionary change, growing interdependence for some and rapid disintegration of old orders for others. America's large purposes must be defined and, to the degree possible, achieved within this rapidly evolving context. A recent report concluded, "The United States . . . has a significant interest in the responsible expansion of an international order based on agreed rules among major powers to manage common global problems, not least those involving the physical environment."[2]

Most immediately, our current age is being defined by terrorism and the United States' response to it, and yet terrorism is not the largest reality of our time. The four revolutions are, and to important degrees terrorism is a reflection of these revolutions, and it is the most vivid, immediate, and the most intense reality. As it is being isolated, prevented, and hopefully crushed, terrorism must not overwhelm other realities, both good and bad, that are most enduring and even more challenging. Though it partially filled a strategic vacuum in the Bush administration, a "war on terrorism" is not a national strategy, and it is not even war in any traditional sense. While managing and hopefully eliminating the terrorist threat to the United States, we should also separately define and pursue our larger, longer-term purposes. If terrorism were magically to disappear tomorrow, most of our challenges would still exist and would require serious, systematic thought and action in the kind of strategic context that does not exist today.

Much of what passes today for "strategy" is in fact ideology. Conservatism is not a strategy. It is a mind-set, a point of view, a system of belief that tells its adherents how to think and too often what to think. The same may be said for other ideologies. They tell you what you should believe. They do not provide a set of large purposes for a great nation and a coherent plan for applying its powers to achieve those purposes. To a different degree, the same is true of the corporate analogy. There is an American myth based upon its capitalist structures that the United States "should be run like a business" and, therefore, that a national strategy is some sort of larger corporate strategy. The analogy fails on many fronts, not least of which is the vast difference between the profit motive, on the one hand, and the pursuit of the public and national interests, on the other, and the different resources available for each. Political parties, businesses, religions, and financial systems all have, or should have, strategies. But in each case these are vastly different undertakings than the process by which the strategy of a great nation is produced.

In setting out America's large purposes in the early twenty-first century, a number of objectives must be kept in mind, including the following: the need to expand our understanding of security; the need to achieve energy security as central to that understanding; the importance of the maritime dimension to larger military strategy; the objective of resisting hegemony abroad without seeking hegemony for ourselves; the importance of encouraging regional leadership by other powers; and our interest in stabilizing fragile states, reducing weapons proliferation, and preventing the militarization of space. These are illustrative of an expanding array of twenty-first-century challenges, almost all of which share the common characteristic of requiring multinational, cooperative solutions.

Within the context of our nation's principles, as well as our traditional powers—economic, political, and military—at least three large purposes should frame an early twenty-first-century national strategy.

To Achieve Security

America's first large purpose is to provide security for its citizens and to do so in ways that expand, not diminish, the security of others and that do not threaten our own constitutional principles. A former national security adviser has said, "Ultimately at issue . . . is the relationship between the new requirements of security and the traditions of American idealism. We have for decades played a unique role in the world because we were viewed as a society that was generally committed to certain ideals and we were prepared to practice them at home and to defend them abroad."[3]

According to the U.S. Commission on National Security/ 21st Century, "For many years to come Americans will become increasingly less secure, and *much less secure than they now believe themselves to be*."[4] Security is not a zero-sum game in which we expand our security at the expense of the security of others. Nor is it exclusively a function, as many suppose, of preventing violence against us. Security will be achievable only if we understand its new dimensions.

Homeland security, a new concept after 9/11, is considered a military, paramilitary, and law enforcement function. Its goal is to take every step to guarantee that further terrorist attacks on America not occur, yet be prepared to respond to them if they do. Genuine security in the twenty-first century, however, must increasingly take on broader meanings. It includes a guarantee of social and economic stability, confidence by the people in their government, opportunity to earn a livelihood, security of the community, security of our natural environment, and a sense of hope for our children's future. America's initial large purpose is to achieve this richer definition of security for all its citizens.

Why richer? Though protected from terrorism, an unemployed American is only partially secure; though protected from terrorism, an American family diseased by pollutants is only partially secure; though protected from terrorism, young people without economic opportunity are only partially secure, and so forth. The one-dimensional Cold War understanding of security—military protection from and deterrence of Soviet missile attacks—is not transferable to a more complex century. Insecurity has many faces, especially in an age of increasing economic uncertainty. So our public discourse, particularly as directed to our large strategic purposes, must accept a much more comprehensive understanding of security.

Like other strategic purposes, domestic security is intimately connected to our nation's ability to achieve its larger purposes in the world. A secure nation, one that is broadening opportunity and hope through constructive growth and expansion, as well as protection against intrusion and attack, is a nation better capable of providing world leadership.

To Expand Opportunity

A second large purpose, therefore, must be to increase domestic economic opportunity to guarantee America's strength in the world. Prosperity and justice at home are directly connected to America's ability to achieve its international purposes, including encouragement of democracy and frustration of destructive forces, particularly the terrorist enterprise. Our economic, political, and military powers are dependent on expansion of domestic opportunity. As our nation grows and expands, we increase our ability to finance our military, secure our society, recapitalize our national assets, invest in public and private projects abroad, and promote our political values. A nation deeply and perpetually in debt is dependent on foreign lenders. A nation where jobs are irretrievably lost is domestically preoccupied and internationally weakened. A nation plagued by corporate fraud is not a nation focused on international markets and investment. A nation suffering declining recruitment and increasing troop attrition due to overextended tours of duty is not, eventually, a strong military power. In short, we cannot disassociate our strength in the world from the health of our domestic economy, the well-being of our citizens, the confidence we have in our government, and our optimism about our future. This point was underscored in April 2000 by a national commission:

> If America does not make wise investments in preserving its own strength, well within 25 years it will find its power reduced, its interests challenged even more than they are today, and its influence eroded. Many nations already seek to balance America's relative power, and the sinews of American strength—social, military, economic, and technological—will not sustain themselves without conscious national commitment. Assuring American prosperity is particularly critical; without it, the United States will be hobbled in all its efforts to play a leading role internationally.[5]

Creating and expanding opportunity cannot be achieved, however, so long as consumption remains the foundation of our national economy. But reliance on consumption in periods of economic turmoil or recession, to the extent citizens are required to buy things whether they need them or not, is to insist on *debt*—personal, corporate, and public. Reliance on debt is reliance on lenders, by definition a status of dependence. Private and public debt in the United States is financed by borrowing from both foreign lenders and future generations. To achieve the large purpose of domestic opportunity and justice, that is, to create economic strength, the foundation of America's economy must shift from consumption to production through saving, investment, and invention. It is telling that, on September 20, 2001, when President Bush sought to rally the nation against terrorism, a centerpiece of that "war" was to spend money, to buy things. The point seemed to be that a strong economy was necessary to counteract terrorism and that the economy could be made strong only by further consumption of goods and services, whether needed or not.

Most economists agree that our revenue codes, our energy policies, our weakening pollution regulations, and our corporate compensation systems, among many other factors, all favor consumption and expenditure over production and investment. Gratification must be immediate, not deferred. To compound the felony, much of our current consumption is financed by borrowing and debt, public, private, and corporate. Personal, and some business, bankruptcies are at an all-time high. We are not producing enough to pay our way. Therefore, we borrow.

Public policies, especially incorporated in the tax laws, can reverse this downward spiral. Tax and other systems can be structured to reward savings and investment and discourage unnecessary consumption. These policies can easily be structured to protect the poor, the elderly, and those on fixed incomes. It is simply a matter of public priorities and our sense of obligation to future generations.

It is a matter of public, if not moral, principle that one generation does not finance its comfort by borrowing from, rather than investing in, the next generation. The power of our principles as a strategic strength is dependent on following those principles at home. To bequeath a legacy of public debt to the next generation—exactly what we are doing now—is a violation of the fundamental principles of a civilized society.

An extension of our effort to create opportunity, and therefore strength, in America must be to expand that opportunity abroad as the antidote for hopelessness and, eventually, resentment of America. Achieving this goal will require the United States to lead and shape the revolutionary forces of globalization. This will require, among other things, continued reduction of protectionism and fundamental recognition of integrated markets and economies under fair rules for protection of workers' rights and sound environmental practice. Increased integration of the economies of the developed world will require that serious consideration be given to forming international market regulatory structures to provide economic stability, protect workers' rights and local environments, prevent market manipulation, and most of all open market opportunities to masses of people without access to them. According to the U.S. Commission on National Security/21st Century, "Thanks to the continuing integration of global financial networks, economic downturns that were once normally episodic and local may become more systemic and fully global in their harmful affects."[6] Currently, globalization is integrating the developed world into regional political entities such as the European Community and regional economic blocs such as the North American Free Trade Agreement (NAFTA) consortium. But it is also widening the gap between trading ("have") nations and nontrading ("have-not") nations. Well over two-thirds of the world belongs to no effective trade bloc.

The United States is the largest direct foreign investor, the largest international borrower, and the largest consumer of international products. It also is the largest national economy in the world and the largest participant in the panoply of multilateral financial institutions such as the World Bank and the International Monetary Fund. Given all these roles, the United States has enormous economic, and therefore political, power in structuring a future global environment that benefits the maximum number in the common interest. Exercise of this power is essential to achieving our second large purpose in the early twenty-first century, expansion of opportunity and therefore hope.

Three challenges stand out. Expanding the benefits of globalization to the less developed world through fair wage and labor rules and environmental protections is one. Increasing opportunities for less-developed countries to trade, and reducing the barriers preventing them from doing so, is another. A third is to establish an international symposium on international market regulations and financial safety nets to stabilize international financial markets. The United States can unilaterally make none of these things happen, but they will not happen at all without U.S. leadership.

To Promote Liberal Democracy

Most would agree that isolationism is not a realistic option for the United States in the twenty-first century. Instant communications, mass travel, integrated markets, large-scale migration, and immigration into the United States, not to say our dominant economic and military power, make us inextricably part of the new world. Any lingering doubt about this reality was eliminated by suicidal terrorist hatred that brought a new kind of warfare to our doorstep. The

United States can either let that new kind of warfare define it and its role in the world, or it can initiate its own role, one defined by our effort to offer opportunity and liberal democracy based on cooperation, internationalism, and law for those who wish them.

Why liberal democracy? This is not to introduce yet another retrograde, and totally unproductive and silly, ideological quarrel. It is a reflection of a simple yet profound observation by Fareed Zakaria, a foreign policy expert, that, as is too often assumed in American discourse, not all democracy is liberal.[7] This is to say that "democracy" is more than reasonably open election of leadership. Painful experience has proved that majorities of voters—such as in Russia, Venezuela, and much of "democratic" Africa—can elect illiberal, authoritarian leaders. Zakaria cogently argues for "constitutional liberalism." In addition to free elections, the conception of liberal in this context includes constitutional guarantees of the rule of law, equality under the law, impartial courts and tribunals, freedom of dissent, protection of private property, separation of state from institutional religion, and protection of diversity and the rights of minorities. The democracy promoted by the United States as one of its large purposes must be, in the classic sense of the word, "liberal" democracy.

As with security and opportunity, promotion of liberal democracy must take into account this revolutionary age. Most particularly, the new political revolutionary reality is the changing nature of nation-state sovereignty. National treasuries and finance ministries can no longer effectively regulate national economies by traditional fiscal and monetary mechanisms. Fluctuating currency exchange rates upset national policies. Location and relocation of major plants can upset whole regional economies. Protectionism can cause, and has caused, nation-state wars and international conflict. National steel, agricultural, and textile industries, as well as entire regional economies, rise or fall on trade policies.

Likewise, the information revolution has made authoritarian governments, including those as large as the former Soviet Union and the People's Republic of China, less tenable. National borders can no longer be sealed and information controlled by propaganda ministries. The Internet, fax machines, international telecommunications and mobile telephones, television, and particularly satellite television have all fundamentally revolutionized information, political and otherwise, in the late twentieth and early twenty-first centuries. In the process, these technologies have undermined national sovereignty, especially in closed systems.

A creation of the Westphalian era, the nation-state has endured for three and a half centuries by guaranteeing security and a degree of economic stability in exchange for its citizens' loyalty. But rapidly evolving world markets will eventually require economic stabilization by international regulation and safety nets very similar to those created in the United States in the wake of the Great Depression. The continued disintegration of some states will require international peacemaking as well as peacekeeping and shared multinational nation-building capabilities. An increased international responsibility for establishing opportunities in the south will be necessary to stem the massive tide of north-south migrations. International epidemics and transnational environmental threats will require greater cooperation on international health issues. The list is long, and "global forces, especially economic ones, will continue to batter the concept of national sovereignty."[8] The world's threats, and its opportunities, are increasingly integrated and transnational and will increasingly require integrated responses that transcend the boundaries of national sovereignty.

The issue is whether the United States, as it should, will undertake the leadership task of using its powers to convert these revolutions to opportunities for the greatest number. Strategically, this is a large purpose indeed. The political challenge is whether the United States and other nations will cede a degree of their national sovereignty to existing or potential international institutions to collectively address new global economic, political, and security realities. This is not a simple proposition. Nations are used to operating independently, absent bilateral or multilateral agreements, and demand the independence to act when, where, and how they alone choose. To grant power to an international institution is to condition, to some degree, a nation's ability to act unilaterally, though most collective agreements contain exceptions for national emergency and the legitimate need for unilateral action.

The integration of global interests will, at the very least, require serious and thoughtful discussion of the nature of nation-state sovereignty when new realities increasingly require collective action and the creation of standing institutions in anticipation of political and economic crises. The issue of sovereignty, the traditional powers inherent in statehood, will be the most significant political question of the early twenty-first century. On an increasing array of matters, nations, including especially a great power such as the United States, will be required to choose between "going it alone" and accepting that "we're all in this together." As the costs in lives and treasure of nation-building, peacekeeping, market stabilization, currency regulation, counterproliferation of weapons, and wars on terrorism and international crime increase, even the United States will feel greater citizen and taxpayer resistance, as has occurred in occupied Iraq, to "go-it-alone" unilateralism. Within four months of declaring victory in Iraq, the United States, reversing course, requested United Nations participation in nation-building. Cold reality will increasingly trump traditional, unilateral exercise of national sovereign power.

In conceptualizing the United States' effort to develop a twenty-first-century strategy, applying all its powers to its large purposes, it might be helpful to visualize a diagram of increasingly larger concentric circles of values, interests, and relationships. Accordingly, the world would be seen in terms of values and interests, as well as geopolitically, as follows: the inner circle would represent America's newly defined larger security; the second circle would represent our established alliances such as NATO; the third circle would represent our participation in international organizations such as the United Nations; the fourth circle would represent our regional relationships such as NAFTA and the European Union; the fifth circle would represent the remaining nations of the world; the sixth circle would represent nongovernmental organizations; and the outer circle would represent nonstate actors, including threats to world order represented by tribes, clans, gangs, terrorists, mafias, and drug cartels.

Schematically, imagine these circles bisected in pie-wedge fashion by three sectors—economics, politics, and military—suggesting the three traditional powers applied in distinct ways to each of the seven circles. The economic sector incorporates the use of power of investment in all its forms. The political sector incorporates the use of the power of diplomacy, economic ties, and alliances in all their forms. The military sector incorporates the real and potential application of force in all its forms. America's principles should permeate and energize the functioning of all three sectors of power and each of the circles of relationships, as well as operate as a considerable constraint on the unprincipled or expedient exercise of those powers.

There could be more, perhaps many more, large purposes than those suggested here. But strategy is not a utopian enterprise. The strategic objective is not to achieve a perfect world or to set out national purposes—for example, elimination of all hunger and disease—beyond any single nation's powers to achieve them. Our large purposes must also not be random; they must relate to each other. Security and the expansion of democracy are enhanced by widespread opportunity. Opportunity is enhanced by security and democracy. All these purposes are enhanced by the others.

Their interrelationship may be described in this way: we must expand our understanding of the notion of security. We must create a productive, expanding society of opportunity and justice to provide the resources necessary to achieve both domestic security and our global objectives. Those objectives include shaping the forces of globalization, using common interests and the common good as a basis for our international relations. And liberal democracy should be expanded within the context of the changing nature of national sovereignty and the extension of global markets.

I have now analyzed the strategic process, identified America's powers and the constraints on those powers, suggested the extraordinary power of principle as an important strategic dimension, and outlined major large purposes toward whose achievement America's powers should be directed. This process now forms the basis for a grand strategy for the United States in the early twenty-first century: *to transform our domestic economy from one of consumption to one of production and, through long-term investment, to recapitalize our education and technology base and achieve energy security; to use the forces of globalization and information to strengthen and expand existing democratic alliances and create new ones; to employ those alliances to destroy terrorist networks and establish new security structures; and, guided by our historic principles, to lead international coalitions in spreading economic opportunity and liberal democracy and in nation-building, counterproliferation of weapons, and environmental protection.*

The next step is to examine the means by which each of America's large purposes can be realized by exercising each of its powers in pursuit of its grand strategy.

4 ✳

Security in the Twenty-first Century

A Larger Understanding

The twenty-first century has already presented itself as an age in which concern for security will be paramount: traditional security against violence, but also security of livelihood, security of community, security of our environment, and security of our children's future. The large purpose toward which United States strategy must be centrally directed is the security of its citizens. A more secure world with expanding opportunities for political participation and economic well-being reduces threats against us and increases America's security. To have the economic, political, and military power necessary for realization of our large purposes, we have to invent new ways to drive progress in our own society.

Revolutionary times require policies that will channel the forces of revolution to our benefit. Against the backdrop of revolution, we must now understand security in terms larger than defense against attack. What are the principles upon which a new national economics might be based to achieve this new understanding of security?

After the terrorist attacks of 2001, Americans have asked how secure their livelihood, their community, their natural environment, and their children's future are. This broader appreciation of security, now added to homeland security, is permeating public discourse. The terrorist attacks of September 11, with all the subsequent talk of homeland security, have led to a reconsideration of what security means in an unstable time. Are new Departments of Homeland Security and Patriot Acts sufficient to produce security when employment, homes, and pensions are lost or are becoming more vulnerable? A new social debate is forming, but traditional politics, locked into old ideological quarrels, is not responding coherently. The elements of a new sense of security must be discussed separately.

Security of the Homeland

The age of terrorism demands that strategy encompass homeland security. On January 31, 2001, the U.S. Commission on National Security/21st Century strongly recommended to President George Bush that a new national homeland security agency be created to restructure and reorganize federal assets to achieve coordination and establish constitutional accountability. Well over a year after the first terrorist attack and two years after that recommendation, such a coordinated agency was finally established. Care must be taken that this not become a domestic Pentagon, a bureaucratic behemoth that crushes initiative and imagination and becomes merely a giant trough for government contracts. A very large coordinated agency can succeed only if it integrates security functions but at the same time rewards individual creative energy. At this moment, that new department is not moving with the sense of urgency it must possess.

Assembled from almost two dozen existing federal offices, the new department has, among its many essential missions, two especially crucial ones: control of our borders and protection of our critical infrastructure—our communications, finance, energy, and transportation systems. Beyond this critical infrastructure are industries such as petrochemicals and food that must also be substantially better protected. The Department of Homeland Security requires three critical integrations: the first is integration of this wide array of existing federal offices and bureaus; the second is the integration of the federal system—national, state, and local governments; the third is the integration of the public and private sectors. Very little progress has been made on the second and third tasks. The "local responders," state and local fire and police, emergency health workers, National Guard, specialized hazardous materials teams, and others, have been neither financed, trained, equipped, nor informed for their new duties. The private sector, companies in the communications, finance, transportation, and energy sectors, as well as the chemical industry, food industry, and others mentioned, should be required to undertake considerably strengthened security measures not only in their own but also in the public and national interest. Well over two years after 9/11, our government has not so instructed them.

The constitutional challenge for the nation is the search for balance between security and liberty. Here the role of the standing military in civil society becomes crucial. The Pentagon has created a new Northern Command, headquartered in Colorado Springs, whose official duties, beyond providing air cover in national emergencies, are as yet unclear. The new command has been tasked with coordinating the role of the military in homeland security. The easiest and most obvious solution is to put the entire mission in the Department of Defense.

There are, however, important reasons that it is not so easy. A review of the constitutional debates of 1787 makes clear that the founders recognized the danger to a republican form of government from stationing full-time soldiers and standing military forces on the streets of our nation. This was a fear that united the often-divided founders. Indeed, it eventually led to the passage in 1878, a hundred years after the founding, of the Posse Comitatus Act, prohibiting the regular military establishment from enforcing the laws of the land. Congress made clear the great difference in a democratic republic between protecting our nation from foreign attack and policing our neighborhoods.

There are new calls that we should "review" this law with an eye to qualifying or even repealing it so that standing military forces would be given the homeland security mission. This would be a mistake of dangerous proportions. Constitutional rights and civil liberties would be in danger from a standing army inside our borders. Short of an emergency of catastrophic proportions and a presidential declaration of martial law, we neither want nor need the Eighty-second Airborne Division on the streets of Cleveland, Boston, or Denver. And, schooled in constitutional principles and history, the vast majority of professional military officers do not want that mission either.

But who, in addition to our public safety agencies, police and fire departments, and emergency health responders, should help respond to an attack and keep the peace and restore order? There is a need for some kind of military capability. Based on their understanding of classical history, our founders once again anticipated the future. They created such an army and called it the militia: citizen-soldiers under the immediate command of the various states, who can be deployed in times of emergency. Since the late nineteenth century these state militias have been known as the National Guard. They were created and given constitutional status as the first responders and the first line of defense in the case of an attack on our homeland.

The U.S. Commission on National Security/21st Century insisted that the National Guard be given the principal mission of response to homeland attack. "We urge, in particular," the commission recommended to the president, "that the National Guard be given homeland security as a primary mission, as the U.S. Constitution itself ordains."[1] The National Guard is composed of citizen-soldiers from all walks of life— teachers, office workers, bankers and businesspeople, nurses and medical personnel—who are or quickly can be trained and equipped for the primary homeland security role. They do not conjure up the danger of military rule so feared by republicans since the Greek city-state.

More than two years after the first major terrorist attacks on America, expert observers almost uniformly believe the United States is prepared neither to prevent nor to adequately respond to the next wave of attacks. America is still at risk and still unprepared.[2] Given this condition, it cannot be said that the elementary level of security, security of life and liberty, has been achieved.

It is difficult to comprehend or explain the absence of urgency in preparing the United State for future terrorist attacks predicted widely by senior intelligence officials and terrorism experts, particularly in the wake of invasion and occupation of a large Arab nation. The range of possible reasons for this lassitude is not large: a belief that war elsewhere is a deterrent to war at home; the presumption that terrorist leadership is disrupted and networks dispersed; a sense that time is plentiful; the complexity of the task; a disbelief in government effectiveness; or simple leadership incompetence.

To all of which reasons responses are obvious. War and long-term military occupation in hotbeds of hostility to the

United States in the Arab and larger Islamic worlds, experts agree, exacerbate rather than dampen the terrorist threat. Osama bin Laden and key al Qaeda leaders and operatives are still at large, and cells are known to exist throughout Europe and quite possibly in the United States. The clock is ticking; almost two years elapsed before stationing of American forces in Saudi Arabia triggered the first bombing of the World Trade Center in 1993. It is complicated to integrate almost two dozen federal agencies, three levels of government, and the public and private sectors; but greater tasks have been carried out in less time when the need, as here, was urgent. Finally, if one is systematically hostile to the notion of government effectiveness, it erodes the urgency of public action; but this hostility does not account for the utter failure to require security in the critical infrastructure owned and operated by private enterprise.

Only history can judge the competence of leaders, but it will surely judge harshly if the United States remains unprepared for the next attack. The current evidence is not encouraging. On September 15, 1999, a national commission warned that America would be attacked by terrorists using weapons of mass destruction and that "Americans will die on American soil, possibly in large numbers."[3] It was ignored by government and the media alike. On January 31, 2001, that same commission recommended to the new president, George W. Bush, that a national homeland security agency be created to consolidate federal resources required to prevent and, if necessary, respond to the predicted terrorist attacks. This recommendation was also ignored. Less than eight months later the United States was attacked, and almost a year and a half then transpired before such a department integrating federal assets was finally established—all in all, not a demonstration of urgency calculated to comfort or inspire confidence.

Even now America's seaports are only beginning to be protected and shipping containers systematically inspected. Land borders are notoriously porous. Petrochemical plants in or near urban areas are spectacularly vulnerable. Energy plants, including nuclear ones, and distribution facilities are relatively unguarded. The National Guard has yet to be trained and equipped for the homeland security mission. Local police, fire, hazardous materials teams, and emergency health responders are just now receiving small amounts of federal financial assistance. Federal, state, and local communications systems and databases have yet to be synchronized. The list goes on.

Where there is no vision—or leadership urgency—the people perish. When attacked once, shame on them: when attacked twice, shame on us.

Security of Livelihood

Even if, however, an achievable degree of homeland security is reached, one cannot be said to be secure if basic requirements of livelihood are denied. We are a capitalist economy, but one in which a large majority of its members has come to accept the role of government in creating and maintaining at least a minimum social safety net required by a civilized society.

If we presume the era of the New Deal, Fair Deal, and Great Society was generally characterized by our national government creating a social safety net for the middle class and the elderly, a ladder of opportunity for the poor, and programs to stimulate rural development and urban renewal, that era ended with the election of Ronald Reagan in 1980. Government, for almost fifty years a vital instrument of growth and progress, became "the problem." and the then hidden strategy of stimulating deficits as a means of reducing government—the "Stockman" strategy ("starving the beast")—become official doctrine.

Now government investment has been replaced by tax cuts, regulation has given way to market forces, and many public social programs, especially for the poor, are replaced by "a thousand points of light," "faith-based charities," and "compassionate conservatism." Perhaps nothing characterizes the current age more than the wholesale demeaning of the word "liberal" and amnesia regarding the half century of social progress it represents.

At the turn of this century, one party resorts to laissez-faire, supply-side economics, and deregulated markets from the 1920s, and the other offers a wide variety of program initiatives focused primarily on the middle class. One ideology claims the country is a meritocracy but ignores the many examples of unequal opportunity; it claims that markets always provide superior solutions but does not acknowledge all the ways in which markets can and do fail. This ideology does enjoy the advantage of consistency. Its economic philosophy has changed little over the past century since powerful interests and financial elites captured its levers of power at the close of the Progressive Era and the age of Theodore Roosevelt.

In an era when government activism is out of favor, the twentieth-century liberal party has resorted to a nebulous centrism—featuring more streetlights and school uniforms—that too readily devolves into a least-common-denominator outcome. Lacking in its economics are central organizing principles or a conceptual framework that gives disparate policy initiatives coherence. In Churchillian terms, "This pudding has no theme."

It is well beyond the scope of this essay to attempt to design detailed new economic, or for that matter foreign and defense, policies. These matters require expert attention at much greater length and in much greater detail than is possible here. For its part, this work is an exercise in strategic concept and framework, and to a degree theory, that does not and cannot seek to fill in all policy and programmatic blanks. It is meant to suggest a *way of thinking* about a revolutionary new present and future, only one of whose realities is terrorism, and even that could well turn out to be symptomatic, not a central or controlling reality. Strategy, the application of national powers to large purposes, is the purpose of this work.[4]

By way of illustration and suggestion, however, certain economic, foreign policy, and defense approaches may be proposed to demonstrate paths that major shifts in thinking may follow, for example, from consumption to an economic framework of production, or from a foreign policy of unilateralism to one of collaborative sovereignty, or from traditional military forces to those more equipped and trained for new kinds of conflict.

The proposed shifts in ways of thinking are meant to be illustrative, not prescriptive, of how a new grand strategy might be pursued through specific new policies. Like alternative policies others may suggest, they should not be used to derail the larger strategic enterprise they are intended to explicate and support.

For example, to respond to the current economic revolutions, our national goal must be security through productivity, fueled by savings and investment, so that every American has the chance to become an entrepreneur, own a home, or afford higher education. For example, a plan to secure America might include a child development account, a citizen savings account, a double Earned Income Credit, and a child care tax deduction patterned after the home mortgage deduction. These initiatives, to replace current massive tax cuts, shift our national priorities from further accumulation of wealth at the top to supporting the vast majority of families in their struggle for economic security, and further shift us from patterns of consumption, whether needed or not, to patterns of productivity required to make us secure.

To expand on this plan, as a national priority children should be put first. Investment in our young people, the mark of a civilized society, should become the nation's highest goal. Children, it has been said, are the message a nation sends to a future it will never see. Every American child should receive necessary health care and the best education possible. If children are the future, America is wealthy enough to invest in that future, and one hallmark of an expanded sense of security is the security of our children's future.

Next, the United States should make its economic foundations secure. Both public and private economic structures must be brought into an accelerating age. The key foundational concepts are long-term investment and accountability. The next highest priority is investment and reinvestment in the nation's most precious assets, its people, and their productivity. It will be necessary for America's corporations, the backbone of capitalism, to reestablish accountability and adapt their own behavior to an age of transparency. The nation's revenue base must be restructured to tax unnecessary consumption and destructive behavior and reward productivity through innovation and investment. And, as central to community security, there should be a new social compact between employer companies and the communities in which their employees live to help provide greater security of livelihood.

Further, our fixed national assets should be recapitalized. We should adopt goal-oriented national budget priorities. This means directing public and private investment toward achieving world leadership in science and technology and recapitalizing our schools, universities, and laboratories. Likewise, it means excellence in education with the goal of America becoming the university of the world. It means rebuilding a modern, productive manufacturing base. It means an efficient national infrastructure and might include, for example, the use of revenue bonds to rebuild aging transportation systems. Genuine security requires a productive nation, the centerpiece of all of America's other large purposes. Let us consider how each of these proposals may contribute to that goal.

Several major initiatives could help make every American family—not just corporate executives, bankers, and lawyers but also Wal-Mart employees and truck drivers—more secure and provide economic opportunity for every child. The initial element of what might be called a Secure America plan is a child development account, a down payment on economic security for a generation of Americans. Every child born in America would receive an account with an initial, tax-free government deposit of $1,000. Parents and family then could continue to contribute to and help manage these funds. After reaching adulthood and receiving instruction in finance management, the owner of the account could use its accumulated capital for higher education, job training, or home purchase or to finance a small business.

The next element of the plan would make every American eligible for Secure America accounts in which our government would match every dollar deposited in this account up to a maximum amount of $1,000. The total amount saved would likewise be available to start a business, buy a home, finance job training, or finance higher education.

An additional element of this proposal would double the Earned Income Credit to a maximum of $8,000 a year for any American working full-time who has a dependent. A portion of this benefit could be extended to all households earning less than $50,000 per year. This benefit could be used to help finance participation in the Secure America account and, thus, be eligible for the government's matching funds.

This security-through-investment plan should also include treating the cost of child care under the tax laws in the same manner as the home mortgage deduction. Quality child care is increasingly a crucial element in the ability of parents to achieve security of their livelihood. This aspect of the Secure America plan would help make quality child care affordable for everyone so that no one would be forced to choose between earning income and caring for his or her children.

Another major national goal should be to focus investment and accountability on securing public and private economic structures. It comes too late to hundreds of thousands of investors and employees who have lost billions of dollars to provide a lecture on the dangers of unregulated or laxly regulated markets. It was clear from any reading of American economic history what would happen when necessary financial regulations are removed. Unscrupulous executives and managers took every advantage of curbed regulatory watchdogs to inflate profits and earnings, cut accounting corners, plunder corporate treasuries, and launch their own gilded yachts.

As usual, however, following the long night of greed comes the dawn of responsibility. Now progressive market regulation is required. Free markets are those in which you are free to make choices, not free to deceive and manipulate. Accounting firms must be forced once again to become public auditors, not collaborating "consultants," and the Securities and Exchange Commission must enforce this standard. Investment banks must provide investors honest assessments of stocks unconflicted by their own underwriting stakes. Boards of corporate directors must be required to do their jobs of overseeing management integrity. And managers must fulfill a mandate of loyalty and duty to their employees and the investing public. These objectives will be achieved only through public regulation. Those who manage the private capitalistic system are periodically required to recognize that the most "free" markets in the world—as, for example, in present-day Russia—are often also the most corrupt. Marketplace corruption contributes to insecurity and undermines strategic strength.

Another crucial intersection of private capital and public regulation is the national revenue system, the taxes paid for public services required by a civilized society. National highways, Social Security systems, public schools, the judicial system, public health systems, the military establishment, and publicly owned natural resources all belong to us, and all require investment of tax dollars to maintain. Every revenue dollar returned to the nation's most wealthy is a dollar not invested in our common wealth and nation. In the private sector, any business executive who runs up large corporate debts in order to artificially inflate stock and return revenues to shareholders, rather than invest in his company's productivity, will not last long. The same practices are equally abhorrent in the public sector. Public assets require public investment.

For most of the last century, our revenue system has been directed toward income. We should now consider, instead, progressively taxing consumption. The capital required for national rebuilding, restructuring, and renewal cannot be accumulated using our persistent low savings rates. While consuming our wealth, we depend on the investments of foreigners to finance our debt and even our defense, sending much of the profits from our own productivity abroad. After a few years of public surpluses and debt reduction, we have now returned to massive deficits and massive borrowing from both foreigners and future generations.

Savings can be increased, productivity modernization achieved, and borrowing, especially from non-Americans, reduced by fundamentally restructuring our revenue system. Instead of mindlessly reducing public revenues in a way that creates huge structural deficits, we should alter *what* we tax in order to enhance economic growth and restore fiscal accountability. Income saved and productively invested should be encouraged and unnecessary consumption taxed.

Practices and habits that hurt our country—pollution, wasteful energy uses, unnecessary plundering of our resources, and our throwaway culture—should be taxed. As 6 percent of the world's population, we consume more than a quarter of the world's energy and produce over a quarter of the world's pollution and trash. Both consumption taxes and pollution taxes would help restore a proper system of public values. Effluents should be taxed and user fees imposed on a graduated basis, and the revenues derived from these sources dedicated to improving children's health.

Additionally, massive tax cuts as economic stimulants will not work so long as the rising cost of health benefits remains the greatest single impediment to job creation. The health care sector represents almost a fifth of our economy. That sector can and should be restructured so that it is more efficient, it provides high-quality, affordable services, more private competition is introduced, and prescription drugs are affordable for all.

Thus, new economic security requires corporate accountability, corporate citizenship, and a tax system based on old-fashioned thrift.

Next, priorities for public investment should now be based on recapitalizing our nation rather than traditional pork-barrel, spoils-to-the-powerful politics. A recent federal study found that, as a matter of national security, America had to recapitalize its education system, especially scientific education, and its university and government laboratories: "the inadequacies of our system of research and education pose a greater threat to U.S. national security over the next quarter century than any potential conventional war that we might imagine. . . . If we do not invest heavily and wisely in rebuilding these two core strengths, America will be incapable of maintaining its global position long into the twenty-first century."[5] Rebuilding our public infrastructure, especially our transportation systems, should be another clear goal. Elevating the United States to the status of university of the world, where we educate not only American young people but also future world leaders, is yet a third.

The goal of making America secure in the turbulent twenty-first century will require new priorities for public investment. A sound economic policy should establish these priorities—scientific leadership, educational preeminence, a highly trained workforce, a productive manufacturing base, and modern, efficient infrastructure, together with preeminent investment in our children. These should be the standards for public investment.

Security of Community

The local community and neighborhood should be restored as the nation's political base unit. *Think globally, act locally* is the well-known mantra. Homeland security and security of livelihood require strengthened community governance. Innovative administration of national social programs—such as public education, welfare, and local security—can be achieved at the neighborhood and community level. Restoring the principles of the Republic—incorporating civic duty and citizen participation—will make communities more secure and the nation's public life more vital.

Although it may seem more a political and social issue, restoration of community government should also be an economic preference. If the national government is, for the time being at least, no longer the instrument of progress and justice, and if we need to restore the classical republican qualities of civic virtue and citizen duty, then reliance on community government is a means of assuring that our national social programs are administered more fairly and justly, and in ways more relevant to local conditions, by American citizens themselves in their local communities.

There is little reason, including that of efficiency, why federally funded and mandated programs of social assistance, environmental quality, public education, workplace safety, public health, and a wide range of other public undertakings cannot be administered by local government councils at least as well as by remote federal bureaucracies. Too often liberals have mistaken means for goals and insisted on federal program administration even as ordinary taxpayers were losing confidence in national administrations. Public trust can be restored and citizen involvement increased by making administration of many federal programs the responsibility of local communities. This can also be achieved without reduction of national standards or federal resources required to meet those standards. Vigorous national commitment to social justice and the common good is perfectly compatible with community activism.

The role of the corporate employer is critical to a community's economic security. Especially since the dawn of the age of globalization, too many corporations have abandoned their role as community citizens and, in pursuit of the quickest profits, closed factories, abandoned workers, and decimated communities. Remote federal bureaucracy is now rivaled by the remote corporate bureaucracy of national chain stores. A new social compact between employer corporations and the communities in which they operate is required. This compact should include guarantees of early notification of intent to close or relocate a plant, paid relocation of at least some workers, individual employee training accounts for new jobs, and cooperation with community governments in alleviating the impact of relocation. Even in an age entranced by deregulation, certain minimum corporate citizenship should be demanded by a modern civil society.

Community security is the centerpiece of national security in the age of terrorism, and local citizens—traditional citizen-soldiers and first responders—will play a much more crucial role in homeland security than ever before. One way to achieve this goal would be to create a United for a Secure America (USA) Citizens Corps trained and equipped for auxiliary homeland security missions, including emergency health response and auxiliary police and fire duties.

With the globalization of economics and an increasing sense that events are beyond their control, the immediate involvement of all citizens can be restored by increasing both their rights and their responsibilities for self-government through their communities.

Security from Energy Dependence

Achieving energy security is a central requirement of national security. "Our dependence on foreign energy is both an economic and a security risk to our country," according to Ambassador Felix Rohatyn.[6] Reducing this risk should become a national goal equivalent to reaching the moon. The

United States has the ability to become sufficiently energy independent that the sacrifice of American lives is never required to obtain foreign oil, especially oil that is used for wasteful consumption. What is lacking is the political will to do so. Our national goals must be sustainability, increased use of renewable resources, and reductions in imported energy. Increased efficiency is also required in national transportation and construction standards. Continued dependence on undependable foreign oil supplies is guaranteed insecurity. The goal of energy security can also be achieved while increasing environmental protection standards.

America's lurching struggle toward a sound energy policy has been neither attractive nor rewarding. Depending on ideology and campaign contributions more than sound science and common sense, it has swung from subsidized domestic production to increased imports, from conventional sources to nuclear fuels, from conservation and fuel efficiency to deregulation and tax incentives for large vehicles, from coal one day to hydrogen the next, and on and on. The current lurch is toward subsidizing the nuclear power industry, which has not put one new plant on line in more than thirty years (due to the costs of construction and inability to compete), and at least $10 billion in tax breaks and subsidies to coal and oil and gas companies, while sharply reducing incentives for renewable alternatives and conservation.

Between 1975 and the late 1980s, fuel efficiency standards for passenger vehicles produced large energy savings. But failure to enact new efficiency standards and tax incentives for larger vehicles has wiped out this trend and sent gas consumption soaring by the 1990s. This despite the fact that "just a 2.7 mile per gallon gain in the fuel economy of this country's light vehicle fleet could displace Persian Gulf imports entirely."[7] Consequently, "The U.S. is likely to be faced with recurring oil and natural gas crises for some years to come. . . . But volatile prices—as with gasoline during the Iraqi war, natural gas last winter, and electricity in 2000—are all but guaranteed. The result is a hidden tax of tens of billions of dollars on American consumers."[8]

With a "war on terrorism" under way in the most oil-rich region of the world, none of this retrograde policy makes any sense, of course, particularly since, as far back as twenty years ago, "a handful of people [terrorists] could shut down three-quarters of the oil and gas supplies of the eastern states without leaving Louisiana."[9] A nation serious about energy security and defeating terrorism would shift dramatically away from massive and wasteful consumption and large-scale concentrated energy production facilities toward intensive efficiency and widely-dispersed sources of energy supply. "We can achieve energy security by using less energy far more efficiently to do the same tasks [while preserving the same quality of life and living standards]—and then by supplying what is still needed from sources that are inherently invulnerable because they're dispersed, diverse, and increasingly renewable."[10] Distributed generation from multiple sources and diverse supplies "makes our electricity infrastructure less vulnerable to terrorist attack, both by distributing the generation and diversifying the generation fuels," according to a current Department of Energy official, who continues, "If you're engaged in this effort . . . you are also engaged in our national effort to fight terrorism."[11] In sum, opportunities to incorporate efficiencies in transportation, home and building construction, appliance performance, lighting, and a host of other uses are growing dramatically and becoming less expensive, especially in contrast to the rapid rise in the cost of constructing traditional concentrated power facilities and the production of energy from fossil fuels and nuclear materials.

The path toward energy security, and therefore security of livelihood, community, environment, and the nation, lies in using energy much more efficiently and dispersing its sources, not in imperial designs in the Middle East supported by massive military occupation and enormous subsidies of a host of new, large-scale conventional power plants.

Even assuming new public-private structures and new budget priorities, the United States will not be economically secure so long as we are energy dependent. "American dependence on foreign sources of energy will . . . grow over the next two decades. In the absence of events that alter significantly the price of oil, the stability of the world oil market will continue to depend on an uninterrupted supply of oil from the Persian Gulf, and the location of all key fossil fuel deposits will retain geopolitical significance," according to a national security report.[12] Energy security is a crucial component of national security, and it must be pursued with the same intensity and commitment of resources used to travel to the moon. This is a national challenge with no single solution. To meet it will require some increase in conventional energy production, for example, of deep gas wells; greater efficiency, especially the adoption of greater transportation efficiency standards; a graduated tax on carbon emissions; increased reliance on renewable energy sources such as sun, wind, and water; and renewed research in alternatives, including hydrogen fuel cells. Properly informed, the American people will adopt this project with the same patriotic vigor and national unity they have exhibited with every national challenge in our history.

The United States must strive to reduce its dependence on foreign sources of fossil fuel energy that leaves this country and its allies vulnerable to economic pressures and political blackmail. Steady development of alternative sources of energy production, and greater efficiencies in energy transmission and conservation, are thus national security as well as economic and environmental necessities.[13]

Here a new tax system can help. By taxing oil imports (with rebates to those who are dependent on those supplies for home heating) and carbon emissions, we would dramatically reduce dependence on unreliable supplies and drastically reduce inevitable loss of American lives fighting for foreign oil supplies. We should also simultaneously shift our declining dependence on imports from the Persian Gulf to Russia. This not only would boost the Russian economy but also would liberate much of our foreign policy in the Middle East.

Forceful political leadership and political will are required. That leadership should be blunt and direct. Right now, America's energy policy is to rely on foreign oil supplies and to go to war for them if they are threatened. We are using our military, that is to say, young Americans, as the guarantor of our wasteful lifestyle. The American people need to be reminded of this: this is our energy policy, and it is immoral.

Security of Our Children

We must hold ourselves accountable to future generations by establishing a sense of public legacies. This accountability can become the new policy standard for all national programs. The vast army of lobbyists seeking immediate favors from our government contains only a tiny platoon speaking for long-term interests and for future generations. Instead, every public undertaking should respond to this question: Will this policy or program affect our children and their children for good or for ill? This standard must particularly apply to the management of our public resources. By accepting a moral duty to future generations, we can assure their security.

As an extension of this philosophy, children can be given priority in current allocation of national resources. Even after twenty years of rhetoric about "family values," 11 million American children have no health care coverage, millions attend dilapidated schools, and almost 20 percent of our young people live in poverty. Millions of children lack quality child care as their parents work, and 10 million children and teens have no supervision after school. Almost 3 million children are abused and neglected, and thousands are murdered or commit suicide. History will not judge this outcome as reflecting true family values.

Instead, a wealthy and secure nation can provide health care, high-quality education, protection, and supervision for every child; and a civilized nation would do so. The U.S. government spends eight dollars per senior citizen for every dollar it spends on our children. More resources must be devoted directly to children, and cancellation of unnecessary weapons systems and cancellation of tax cuts for the rich would help pay for this urgent priority. Immediate health care coverage for all children, protection and supervision for every child, community-based day care and after-school supervision, and guaranteed access to quality preschool for every child should be among a productive nation's highest priorities. In addition to the proposed child development account and the child care tax deduction outlined earlier in this chapter, a wage supplement program for early childhood educators, presently compensated at poverty-level wages, should be adopted to attract high-quality, accredited teachers into the earliest childhood education.

The notion of public legacies must be incorporated into our thinking. A new standard for a secure political economy should be the impact of today's policies on tomorrow's generations. Each generation should receive a healthy planet and a healthy economy. But a consumer culture, with its emphasis on immediate gratification and the newest product, represents a gigantic tax on future generations—a tax of pollution, congestion, waste, and depletion. Instead, all public, and hopefully much private, dealings should take into account how they will affect our children and generations of Americans to come.

Most Americans, in managing their personal finances, go to great lengths through their wills and estate planning to secure some kind of private legacy to their children. Why should not this same kind of forethought also go into our public legacies? We not only leave property and possessions to our children. We also leave a public legacy of our environment, our resources, our public safety, our national policies and values. What good is a large private estate if our heirs cannot breathe the air or drink the water?

Such a commitment to generational equity also necessitates addressing the public financing challenges that threaten the economic security of future generations. For years now we have known that the growing costs of the two largest government programs—Social Security and Medicare—will consume an ever-increasing share of the budget, pushing out what is left for the important public investments described earlier. To ensure that future retirees live with some dignity and that huge projected deficits be controlled, changes that do not affect current retirees must be phased in. Those changes may include flexible retirement ages or indexing Social Security benefits to reflect longer life expectancies. But, unless trillions of dollars of debt are bequeathed to future generations, change we must.

Investing in the security of our public heritage does more than benefit us; it is the right thing to do for our children. As a matter of national values and political economics, intergenerational accountability, a commitment to future generations to leave behind a better world in every respect than the one that was inherited, is necessary. Only with this kind of accountability will future generations also be as secure as the current generation wishes itself to be.

Central to the United States exercising its powers to achieve its large purposes—the touchstone of strategy—it must guarantee those powers by the strength of its internal systems, and strengthening those domestic systems then becomes its primary large purpose. The world's leading republic is only as strong as its economic, political, and military powers permit, and those powers are the product of a dynamic, expanding, and secure nation. America's strategic role in the world can be guaranteed only to the extent its principal large purpose—providing security for its own people—is realized.

Central also to every great power pursuing its strategy, however, is a clear sense of who and what it is. This is a crucial issue that the United States must directly and straightforwardly address at this turning point in its history.

5 ✳

Principled Engagement

Expanding Security through Opportunity

How should the United States apply its powers—in keeping with its principles—to achieve its large purposes abroad? In the case of America's relations with its international neighbors, application of its political powers, to include diplomacy, alliances, agreements, and coalitions, is a place to start.

We are now more than a decade beyond the Cold War, and we have failed to arrive at a comprehensive sense of America's role in the post–Cold War, early twenty-first-century world. For almost half a century our central organizing principle, upon which both foreign policy and defense policy were built, was containment of communism. The world in which we now live defies the simplicity and predictability such a doctrine offered. And even containment of communism left unanswered the question of *how* to contain communism, a question that often divided our country deeply, not least between those, such as Henry Kissinger, advocating the use of power to promote our interests and those, such as Jimmy Carter, advocating adherence to human rights as defining of our values.

Rather than presenting a new foundation and framework to define America's role in the world, the current administration has embarked on a mission to apply power without particular reference to America's principles. Or rather, it might be more accurate to say, its announced purpose for application of military power through preemptive action seems to be that America has an obligation (perhaps divine?) to impose good and eradicate evil. American history offers little precedent for this presumed theocratic foreign policy principle. Its justification is the war on terrorism. Its doctrine is that we are powerful enough to do as we wish, and those who are not with us are against us. As we are finding to our surprise and frustration in our occupation of Iraq, a world sharply divided between pro- and anti-Americans is not a world in which even a semblance of security is achievable.

Moreover, the administration's preoccupation with military force as a first, rather than a last, resort erodes our greatest strength—the admiration the world has for the American character and for American economic and political systems. We drive the world's prosperity. We are the champions of the ideal of democracy. We are the world's greatest source of optimism, energy, and hope. Global citizens by the hundreds of millions say that, while they disagree, sometimes violently, with the U.S. government, they respect and admire the American people. To compromise that reservoir of personal goodwill through belligerence is to squander one of our most powerful resources.

Historically, we are a revolutionary nation that has been at its best when it applied its character of innovation and adaptability to the challenges of changing times. Given our revolutionary heritage, we should welcome, not resist, innovation and experimentation by other nations rather than be seen as reactionary and antagonistic to change. And we are a democratic republic whose government powers are checked and balanced by a written constitution.

When we act outside these definitions of our character, for example, when we exhibit the characteristics of an imperial power, a hegemon, or a global constable, whether in Iraq or elsewhere, or when we resort to manipulation, deceit, or intrigue in our dealings with other nations, which we did repeatedly in the Cold War, we become some other kind of nation than who we claim to be. And when we do so, we always pay a price. Indeed, we *diminish* our authority as a world leader when we abandon our ideals or violate our principles.

Based on these principles that define us, American foreign policy should articulate the United States' grand strategy in the twenty-first-century world.

Standards and Goals for Global Conduct

Within the context of the several large purposes of achieving security, creating opportunity, and promoting liberal democracy, a number of specific goals—the detailed objectives dictated by our large purposes—suggest themselves. We wish to maintain friendly relations with all nations of goodwill through open trade and honest diplomacy; we also seek to foster a stable world community characterized by opportunity and human rights for the greatest number and a minimum of violence; we seek to subdue destructive forces and prevent proliferation of the weapons they use; we wish to promote stewardship over and generational accountability for our universally shared natural environment, the oasis in boundless space upon which we all depend; we seek to organize a new security environment to defeat forces of state disintegration and non-state terrorism and preserve the well-being and security of Americans at home and abroad; and, finally, we wish actively to engage in and where possible lead the world community without unnecessary entanglement in ancient quarrels and grievances.

In achieving our large purposes and realizing these objectives, the following standards should guide our conduct in the world:

Our alliances, both old and new, should be characterized by equality of status, common interests, and greater shared responsibilities. And participation in these alliances should not require us to compromise our principles.

With our allies we must seek to prevent the failure of states or, if they fail, seek to manage their peaceful restructuring.

We must explore new areas where international cooperation may relieve disproportionate burdens on U.S. economic and military resources.

We must resist imperial designs by others without seeking empire for ourselves.

Our military power should be used only to defend our nation, protect our justifiable interests, fulfill our alliance commitments, and prevent imminent and unavoidable attack.

Our new definition of security must be adapted to an age in which the nature of conflict is rapidly evolving.

Our economic strength, arguably our greatest traditional strength, should be used to help expand both opportunity and open societies for those nations left behind.

Finally, we should encourage liberal democracy—especially among regional powers that may act as models in their regions—including forms of democratic government possibly different in design and structure from our own.

Democracy and Political Power

America's alliances must be based on more than the presence of common enemies and must increasingly require more equitable sharing of the burden of maintaining stability. Throughout the Cold War our practice of expediency was based on the belief that the enemy of our enemy was our friend. It led us, for example, to support a corrupt and repressive regime in Iran until the Shah fell in 1979, and then to support an even more dangerous regime in Baghdad in a 1980s war against Iranian militants who dethroned the Shah. If that policy of expediency ever served our larger purposes, it no longer does so. Further, a policy based on expediency is against our principles. The same may be said of U.S. support for a military coup in Chile against a democratically elected government, the overthrow of the Mossadegh government in Iran, and repeated assassination attempt against Fidel Castro and other national leaders. Our actions will be either guided by the ideals of a democratic society or discredited by a carefully observing world.

In our recent war against Iraq, we formed alliances with countries like Yemen whose head of state, Ali Abdullah Salleh, was busily importing Scud missiles from North Korea and trading weapons throughout the region. This same "ally" sided with Iraq in the previous Gulf War and currently refuses to let us investigate militant groups believed to harbor al Qaeda cells in his country. He exhibits none of the qualities that define democratic leaders. Yet he became our new best friend for one simple reason—he let us use his territory for military purposes. The price to be paid once the dogs of war are chained, both in compromise of our principles and in the substantial cash we are undoubtedly paying him, has yet to come due.

Nowhere is that price more evident than in Iraq itself, which we willingly supplied with the capability to manufacture biological and chemical warfare agents in the 1980s. After the first Persian Gulf war, UN arms inspectors found quantities of chemicals and missile parts labeled with the names of American companies such as Union Carbide and Honeywell. A recent news report stated:

> The story of America's involvement with Saddam Hussein in the years before his attack on Kuwait—which includes large-scale intelligence sharing, supply of cluster bombs through a Chilean front company, and facilitating Iraq's acquisition of chemical and biological precursors—is a typical example of the underside of U.S. foreign policy. It is a world in which deals can be struck with dictators, human rights violations sometimes overlooked, and accommodations made with arms proliferators, all on the principle that "the enemy of our enemy is our friend."[1]

That is indeed a foreign policy principle. It just happens not to be an American one.

While resisting the sacrifice of principle to expediency, we must make our alliances not only more respectable but also more relevant to the new realities of our age and more consistently guided by democratic principles. Now our most important alliances, such as NATO, must be built on equitable sharing of both benefits and burdens. NATO was formed to contain communism behind the Iron Curtain. One of our most important international objectives should be to give

NATO a new and more relevant purpose. That purpose might well evolve into a peace*making* commitment on the borders of Europe—such as in the Balkans—and beyond and the creation of special purpose forces to carry out that mission. We must redefine the common interests that cause us to continue to ally. If NATO is to accept a peacemaking role, areas of vital interest, command structures, and relative contributions must all be spelled out in advance of a crisis.

There is a substantial difference between peacemaking and peacekeeping. Peace*making* is the use of offensively trained and equipped intervention forces to enter a conflict environment and halt hostilities. Peace*keeping* is the use of defensively trained and equipped forces to maintain the peace once it is achieved. Critics of UN peacekeeping efforts rarely recognize that troops defensively trained and equipped are doomed to fail in an environment of intense conflict.

We should consider, for example, creation of a NATO intervention force with several missions: keeping the sea-lanes of communication open; protecting the flow of oil supplies; and dealing with any force that might want to block international commerce or exact some tribute for the open usage of any of the world's critical maritime straits. Over the years, this mission could then develop into a full-blown international peacemaking force. Likewise, considerable discussion has focused on a UN peacemaking capability, one that might operate independently of or in tandem with a similar NATO force.

This is but an illustration of further ways in which twentieth-century alliances need to be more relevant to twenty-first-century realities. According to a security panel, "Not every such problem [of weak and failed states, ethnic separatism and violence, and crises they breed] must be primarily a U.S. responsibility, particularly in a world where other powers are amassing significant wealth and human resources."[2] One of the components of a twenty-first-century foreign policy based on expanded opportunity is to strengthen regional powers. Russia, China, and India are key nations in their regions and are becoming so in the wider world. The success of democratic evolution in these nations will be crucial to regional and world stability. Because of both their size and their importance in their respective regions, the U.S. Commission on National Security/21st Century gave as one of its most important recommendations to the new Bush administration that we should "assist the integration of key major powers, especially China, Russia, and India, into the mainstream of the emerging international system."[3] In addition, we should encourage greater regional leadership roles for each. Democracy is still taking root in Russia and has yet to develop in China; its failure to develop in either giant nation would have profound implications for the United States and the world.

North Korea offers a particularly vivid example where China might help lead—as it has begun to do—in regional isolation of, and collective negotiation with, a nation that endangers East Asian security more than it does ours. If we are unable to convince states neighboring outlaw nations such as North Korea that their interests are at stake in isolating and resolving threats, then we are in for a long century. The threat of North Korea also underscores the first principle that alliances should be properly formed. North Korea received much of its recent nuclear technology from Pakistan, our ally in Afghanistan. True allies do not let their immediate self-interest endanger their partners. Nor can we afford to expediently turn a blind eye toward dangerous behavior in one venue, such as North Korea, in order to obtain support in another, such as Afghanistan.

Only recently, prominent conservative voices were heard predicting inevitable military confrontation with China. The implications of that policy are difficult to imagine. Rather, our belief in the therapy of capitalism should lead us to encourage forces of democracy in China and its emergence as a stabilizing force in the region. Firmness, consistency, and respect will trump bellicosity every time.

Likewise, Russia can and should become a major Western nation and a major oil exporter, in partnership with Western production companies, to replace unstable supplies in the Persian Gulf and reduce OPEC's leverage on the United States. Further, Russia must become a stable partner in the Western economic and political world—including membership in NATO—as soon as possible. "Part of the process of building a larger zone of peace involves also engaging Russia and drawing it into a closer relationship simultaneously with Europe and with the Euro-Atlantic community," argues Zbigniew Brzezinski.[4] And India's vast technological potential can energize a regional information revolution and help position that nation as an economic and political leader in the region.

Finally, the nature of sovereignty will change in the twenty-first century under the pressure of globalization, and events may require selective delegation of sovereignty to international organizations newly designed to *make* the peace where violence erupts, to regulate weapons production and proliferation, or to regulate currency and financial markets to prevent imminent collapse. Care must be taken not to abrogate traditional nation-state sovereignty unnecessarily or lightly. But events may provide no alternative but to create new, carefully constructed international regimes to prevent collapse or chaos.

Multilateral peacemaking will be an increasing global requirement. As previously noted, peace*making* requires offensively trained and equipped forces—multilateral because no single nation, including the sole superpower, could or should possess or wish to possess the capability to police the world, and offensive because peacekeeping forces cannot keep the peace where none exists.

Additionally, the time may come—and soon—when international institutions are required to coordinate the stabilization of markets and currencies, further integrate central bank actions, and regulate international commerce. Globalization will increasingly require coordination of macroeconomic, antitrust, banking and securities regulation, and even tax policies. To these add such human policies as the environment and public health. Other collaborative tasks may be undertaken by new regional entities and even coalitions of the willing.

There will be increasing occasions in which circumstances and common sense require that we must pool our sovereignty to implement programs of peacekeeping, nation-building, third world development, counterproliferation of weapons, and standards of justice. The more we ignore the imperatives of this new reality, the more we hoard our sovereignty, then the more isolated we will become, the more we will be tempted to resort to our own force, and the less sovereignty we will have left to protect.

Security and Military Power

As a matter of principle, and recognizing its republican history, the United States must not seek empire in the Middle East or elsewhere. According to published reports, senior officials in our current government previously proposed that we create a permanent U.S. military presence in occupied Iraq to intimidate Iran and Syria, buffer Israel, and replace Saudi oil with Iraqi oil. Any such grandiose notion of playing hegemon in the greater Middle East region is folly and a prescription for disaster. Its political and financial costs are unknown and probably unknowable. Though not until July 2003, almost three months after the fall of the Baghdad government, did the U.S. government admit that American military forces in support of U.S. governors and administrators would remain in Iraq for at least five years at the cost of at least $1 billion per month and an unknown number of American lives.[5] As attacks against U.S. forces, UN aid missions, and infrastructures continue, that occupation could well approach a decade and the size of the U.S. military presence expand, increasing the costs dramatically. The political reality of mounting citizen opposition may well bring these grand imperial dreams back to earth.

This scheme of remaking the Middle East to our liking, never presented as such to the American people, represents a secret dream of empire and is contrary to America's traditional principles. This is, no doubt, the reason it was never publicly discussed as our official policy. Secret policy is inevitably bad policy.

Without knowing what our larger purposes are in the region, suspicions legitimately arise when rumors of empire drift through the salons of Washington. We are assuming responsibility to reconstruct Iraq, referee its bitter ethnic quarrels, bear the cost for rebuilding a nation of 22 million, and place tens of thousands of American service personnel in jeopardy for an untold number of years. But constant attrition of American forces from guerilla warfare may eventually cause us to retreat from the rubble and let Iraq devolve into a sinkhole of tribal violence on CNN. And here the difference between the narrow "strategy" of preemption and the vastly more comprehensive notion of grand strategy becomes apparent. According to the British strategist B. H. Liddell Hart:

While the horizon of strategy is bounded by the war, grand strategy looks beyond the war to the subsequent peace. It should not only combine the various instruments [powers], but so regulate their use as to avoid damage to the future state of peace—for its security and prosperity. The sorry state of peace, for both sides, that has followed most wars can be traced to the fact that, unlike strategy, the realm of grand strategy is for the most part terra incognita—still awaiting exploration, and understanding.[6]

America's struggle to extricate itself from Iraq and its "sorry state of peace" is painful testimony to the fact that the national security strategy based on preemptive war was not part of a grand strategy one of whose large purposes was to achieve and maintain "a future state of peace."

A democratic form of government such as ours requires consent of the people for their nation's policies and the obligations in lives and treasure those policies require before, not after, invasion of foreign nations. When the informed consent of the people is neither sought nor given, policy is bound to fail when harsh reality replaces grandiose, and usually secret, schemes.

American military power must be used judiciously and prudently, even more so now that we are the dominant military power on earth by several orders of magnitude. We now spend more each year on our military establishment than at least the next five major powers, including China, Russia, and the United Kingdom combined, and it is estimated that in the next decade the United States will put more of its wealth into its military establishment than *all* the rest of the world combined.

Our forces must be used primarily to protect our legitimate security interests and those of our allies. When they are deployed abroad, certain standards must be clearly stated and met. We must define our political and military objectives, and our political goals must be tangible, obtainable, and stated in concrete terms. The American people must support the use of our forces in any sustained military operation and must be fully cognizant of the proposed levels of military force and the potential costs, including in human lives. Our military forces should be committed only after diplomatic, political, and other means of conflict resolution have been exhausted and after local forces are determined to be insufficient to resolve the conflict. At least within governing and policy-making circles, we must be clear on how we intend to achieve our objective and what strategies, tactics, and doctrines we mean to employ. Command structures must be clearly defined, and our plan of operation must be simple and achievable in its execution.[7]

There are few if any security reasons that the American people—to whom the American military belongs—cannot be better satisfied that these conditions have been met before going to war in Iraq or elsewhere. The principle at stake here is openness and honesty with the American people, whose sons and daughters fight our wars. History has repeatedly taught us, not least in Vietnam and quite possibly in Iraq, that failure of full disclosure of possible costs in lives and taxes of a proposed military operation is a prescription for erosion of public confidence when circumstances turn against us and, in turn, becomes a prescription for political disaster. It is axiomatic that a policy that cannot be disclosed honestly is a policy that cannot succeed.

We must, with our allies, either seek to prevent or prepare for state failure. We and our allies did not do so in Yugoslavia, and hundreds of thousands of people suffered from that neglect. Like Yugoslavia, Iraq, Jordan, and Saudi Arabia are artificial concoctions thrown together to satisfy European ambitions and competitions following World War I. Preparation must be made to manage their restructuring if the seams fail, especially in Iraq. The penalty for unwillingness or inability to anticipate state failure is harsh.

Iraq stands as the most immediate example of the threatened problem of a vanquished state. An American military proconsul running the country for more than a few months invites remnant Republican Guard units to lay siege to the American emperor's palace—a drumbeat already too familiar. But postwar Iraq does not stand alone. Congo and Nigeria, and even potentially Pakistan, represent immediate examples where the humanitarian consequences of state failure are staggering and, therefore, geopolitical. And Afghanistan, whose liberation seemed easy at the time, is proving less easy to pacify and democratize. A Taliban resurgence underscores the reality of long-term U.S. military occupation in a conquered tribal, theocratic, or authoritarian nation (in this case all three) during the painfully slow process of structuring democratic institutions. One generation is often not sufficient.

Whether the United States likes it or not, this burden—the human costs of war (Liddell Hart's "sorry state of peace")—must be calculated and borne when we invade a country or when a state for which we have assumed responsibility fails. Whether we call it "nation-building" or something else, the United States will eventually be required to enlist the greater democratic world in anticipating the collective burden of supporting fragile states or restructuring those that fail or that we cause to fail. It is difficult, as we have seen, to organize the international community to help nations rebuild in those instances where we have acted alone or with narrow support in overthrowing existing governments against the opinion of the world community.

As the nature of conflict evolves, an expanded concept of security is required. An advocate of military reform for the past twenty years, I now argue for the application of reform principles to American diplomacy—new strategies, new doctrines, and new ways of structuring relationships. Security will be achievable only if we deny the basic resources of money, weapons, sanctuary, and recruits to new forces of violence—mafias, pirates, most of all terrorists and other "nonstate actors." New kinds of threats will require new kinds of resistance—paramilitary and special forces especially trained and equipped to deal with quasi-criminal forms of warfare.

But security will increasingly take on extramilitary dimensions, such as opportunity for economic growth, stability of communities and cultures, adaptability of disparate countries to the new age of information and globalization, and possibly even evolution of new forms of democratic government. More expansive definitions of security will require more expansive means of achieving them—means of diplomacy, of economic growth, and of dispersed investment more immediately beneficial to dispossessed people than to already wealthy elites.

Opportunity and Economic Power

In using our economic strength to offer opportunity and hope in the less developed world, we can start with refugee camps and nonfunctional economies where well over a billion people live on less than a dollar a day, and 3 billion people live on less than two dollars a day. Though we cannot, by ourselves, alleviate the suffering of these impoverished masses, we can help create international institutions that can begin to do so by bolstering infrastructure construction—particularly water resources development, microloans for the financing of shelter and income creation, assault on diseases such as AIDS and malaria, universal global literacy, and agricultural development sufficient to provide an adequate level of nutrition.

Traditional "top-down" foreign aid should be replaced by new grassroots methods of creating economic opportunity. Microlending programs in Asia and Latin America offer particular hope for a new approach to development. The needs of women in the developing world also must especially be addressed. Through such avenues as education, microlending, agricultural technology, and property rights, empowerment of women—especially mothers—improves children's health, education, and nutrition and lifts the conditions of society at large.

Corporate America should enlist in the struggle for global economic opportunity. Though some U.S. businesses have been forces for global progress, overall American companies have reflected their country's international policy values and objectives either voluntarily or not at all. In the future, American companies should set humane standards against child and slave labor, for improving worker rights, and for eliminating environmental damage in the developing world. By establishing standards of conduct, for example, as with the Foreign Corrupt Practices Act prohibiting bribery and corruption of local officials, U.S. commercial interests have demonstrated that they can, in most cases, be competitive even while representing higher principles. American corporations, representing American interests, should be as good citizens abroad as they are at home, for corporate America, like the U.S. government, is judged by its behavior, and we Americans are all judged by the behavior of both.

Finally, to use our economic power to win the world to our cause and replace hopelessness with opportunity, American markets must be opened to the products of the world's poorest people. Protection against these products hurts American consumers and foreign workers and sets back the march of democracy. We must continue to be global leaders in expanding world trade through demonstration of principles of openness and equality of treatment.

An international policy of expanded opportunity and liberal democracy based on the proposition that we are all in this together may be called cooperative, internationalist, multilateral, or any one of a number of similar terms. It may be ad hoc and event driven, or it may be more permanently structured around common goods, as well as common threats and enemies, and ratified by treaty, agreement, or alliance. To a degree, how nations of the world cooperate is determined by pragmatic considerations, in other words, by what works.

But if goals, such as raising global living standards through expanded opportunity, nation-building, counterproliferation of arms, or institutionalizing security and stability through expanding the reach of liberal democracy, are long-term, sweeping in scope, and comprehensive in their involvement, structured institutions with some degree of authority, if not sovereignty, are required. This issue, once again—national sovereignty versus collective action—will emerge as one of the dominant political questions of this century.

The choices for the United States are finite. One is to act unilaterally. Another is to form ad hoc coalitions of the willing. Another is to involve existing international institutions such as the United Nations. The final choice is to devise new institutions not yet known or tried. Oddly, the U.S. operations in Iraq have involved all but the fourth option. We announced our willingness to act unilaterally. We finally received some support from Great Britain and very nominal support from a few others—none major allies. Then, very shortly, intractable politics, staggering costs, and guerilla resistance required us to turn once again to the UN for help, all within the space of six months.

The alternative argued for here is an *anticipatory* internationalist policy (that is, one that does not wait for crises to arise) based on collaborative sovereignty, the collective decision by nation-states to aggregate their sovereignty to deal with both threats and opportunities in a structured way that benefits the interests of all. If we want to lead the world, we must stay engaged in and ahead of the world in a way that respects the people of the world.

6 ✳

The New Security and the
Use of Military Power

Thus far, this essay has considered ways in which the United States may deploy its economic and political power to define a new role in a new world. Consideration must now be given to the uses of military power to achieve its strategic objectives—its large purposes.

Great powers throughout history have successfully maintained their status over time only when they possessed the genius to imagine, and the will to pursue, a systematic plan to dedicate the means they possessed to the achievement of large national purposes. Lacking a grand strategy, the United States is today seen by too many peoples of the world as a great power without purpose—a giant that pronounces rather than listens—and thus as a great danger.

Without understanding the impact of the four simultaneous revolutions—globalization, information, and change in the nature of both sovereignty and conflict—a search for national security is futile. To respond to the first two revolutions requires foreign policy initiatives in the Middle East and elsewhere as bold as the Marshall Plan and as encompassing as energy security. To create a national security strategy requires an understanding of the changing nature of conflict particularly, and that requires an understanding of the erosion of the sovereignty of nation-states.

Revolution in Conflict

For 350 years, wars have been fought between the uniformed armies of nations with fixed borders, meeting in the field to achieve a political result. Rules evolved for these wars: Geneva conventions and a body of international law spell out the norms for humane treatment and repatriation of prisoners, the rights of noncombatants, rules against the use of torture, and so forth. But twenty-first-century warfare already looks dramatically different. Nations disintegrate; and when a nation disintegrates, as in the former Yugoslavia, geographic borders warp and sometimes evaporate. Indeed, part of the process of creating peace among ethnic combatants in a disintegrating nation involves drawing new boundaries and building new nations. And now, in the new age of terrorism, we experience violence being perpetrated by combatants in civilian clothes, representing no nation, attacking civilian targets, with no political agenda, and possessing only a fanatical commitment to destruction for its own sake.

When the nature of conflict changes, the means of assuring security must also change. New forms of violence resemble war, but by historic standards they are not. They resemble crime, but they are not. What is this new conflict, and how should we deal with it? We call much of this new kind of violence terrorism. But labeling every bad actor a terrorist tempts us to embrace wretched allies on the always-dubious theory that the enemy of our enemy is our friend. On this same theory, we supported undemocratic and repressive authoritarian oligarchies during the Cold War simply because they were opposed to communism. We set about assassinating foreign leaders we did not like. The bills we accrue from despicable allies and unprincipled policies that undermine the very principles we claim to defend, however, *always* come due.

In the past ten years, we have seen a dozen or more low-intensity conflicts between tribes, clans, and gangs. We participated in some, including in Somalia, where we experienced the painful consequences of brawling, however well intentioned, in another man's alley—as memorialized in the film *Black Hawk Down.* We passively observed similar bloody conflicts, in Rwanda and elsewhere, where the weapon of choice, a machete, dated to the Bronze Age. We successfully formed a "coalition of the willing," essentially an ad hoc international posse, in Bosnia, Kosovo, and Kuwait. We earned a quick victory in Kuwait largely due to intensive bombing and maneuver warfare. But, with that exception, post–Cold War conflict has been characterized by nonstate actors (tribes, clans, and gangs), "nonarrayed" enemies (those not presented in traditional battle formation) representing "asymmetrical" threats—using ingenuity, not strength, to bypass our military might. Because they did not follow historical conventions, late twentieth-century wars have seemed to some unfair and somehow more barbaric than conflict has been throughout history, as for example in post-"victory," occupied Iraq. According to one survey:

> Foreign crises will be replete with atrocities and the deliberate terrorizing of civilian populations. . . . The type of conflict in which this country will generally engage in the first quarter of the 21st century will require sustainable military capabilities characterized by

stealth, speed, range, unprecedented accuracy, lethality, strategic mobility, superior intelligence, and overall will and ability to prevail.[1]

Yet, innovations in violence can be achieved by weaker forces. Nowhere was this more evident than on September 11, 2001, when nineteen suicidal men in civilian clothes using e-mail, the Internet, elementary flight instructions, and tradesmen's tools converted kerosene-burning commercial aircraft into weapons of mass destruction, manned missiles, against civilian targets. There was an evil genius about it. It was a shocking initiation into the twenty-first century, so shocking that it left some with the naïve belief that it will never happen again or that, if it does, it will not be in their cities. But few seriously believe that the bin Ladens of the world are done with us.

Our massive military and technological superiority did not protect us from this nonstate, nonarrayed, asymmetrical, iconoclastic new form of conflict. Technology may in fact have seduced us into assuming security. While we pour enormous amounts of capital into national missile defense—trying to hit a bullet with a bullet—our enemies turned our own technology against us. Faith in technology should not blind us to the necessity of innovation in the age of the transformation of war; faith in technology must not handcuff our imagination and lull us to sleep.

We are now trying to force new forms of conflict into traditional categories so that we can try to understand and respond to them. Our response to the first terrorist attack was to declare "war on terrorism." But what should have been a two-front war, abroad and at home, is being fought on one front only. We have made war in Afghanistan and Iraq while badly neglecting homeland security. The urgency demonstrated by the Iraq invasion has not been present at home.

So far in Afghanistan, our military has replaced a repressive theocracy with a less repressive, but still tribal, form of government. Even so, the Taliban is resurgent, and al Qaeda cells still operate throughout the Arab world, in Europe, and even in the United States. Further, we invaded Iraq without adequate preparation—as the Council on Foreign Relations' report of October 2002 documented—for what experts believe would be inevitable retaliatory attacks on the United States from radical fundamentalist groups.[2] Thus, it is far too early to declare victory in this war.

Meanwhile, the "warriors" rounded up in this conflict and detained at Guantánamo Bay, Cuba, are denied warrior status. They are also denied criminal status and thus the rights inherent in our criminal justice system. If they are not warriors, and they are not criminals, what are they? The answer is consequential in that it may contain a clue to the broader question of how to define security in the age of this new conflict. We do not know what to call the "detainees" because we do not know exactly what they have done. The Taliban constituted a theocratic regime that harbored an anti-Western, antidemocratic, antiliberal radical fundamentalist terrorist group. Are the Taliban warriors part of a national army, or are they criminals? Or are they something else? The closest our government has come so far are "enemy combatants." Perhaps they are combatants of the future. Will conflict in the twenty-first century resemble more the high-tech games of Star Wars or the bloody, ruthless, barbaric combat of the twelfth-century Assassins?

If a return of the Assassins is the wave of the future, this has dramatic consequences for how we define security and how we seek to achieve it. There are two basic schools of thought, among a wide array, about dealing with terrorism. One school believes the threat is inevitable and that we should crush it, including preemptively, in places like Iraq; it also believes that "evil" nations, dictatorships possessing weapons of mass destruction, should be folded into the war on terrorism. The other believes that we should try to understand the nature of the threat with considerably more thoughtfulness and, to the degree possible, reduce its causes and isolate its irredeemables. The first school of thought has the virtue of simplicity, and, while force is periodically required, the second has the much greater chance of ultimate success.

Limits of Preemption

The preemption approach has profound long-term foreign policy consequences. For example, in Afghanistan, we armed the mujahadeen to fight the Soviets in the 1980s. Then, when the Soviets left, we departed, and the Taliban took over and eventually provided hospitality to al Qaeda. Now we have returned to depose the Taliban, whom we once supported. For a great power capable of prevailing in most wars, management of the peace—establishing liberal democracy and expanding opportunity—is often more important and more problematic.

This new century requires a much clearer understanding of new threats and the causes of those threats than we have so far seemed interested in pursuing. Who exactly is our enemy, and why does he hate us? Unlike the clear-cut twentieth-century ideological struggle between democracy and communism, the role of poverty, disease, and despair becomes much more central. The role of cultural difference also becomes more crucial—"Take your filthy movies and go home," cry those who resent us and our popular culture. And the role of resentment—of our wealth, of our power, of our willful and wasteful consumption of resources, of our arrogance, and of that popular culture—becomes a much greater political factor.

We have witnessed the power of resentment in Iraq, whose people we liberated from a tyrant. What benefits that liberation provided were soon overwhelmed by the deterioration in the structures of ordinary life and the failure of basic social services. Overnight, liberators became occupiers who could not even read street signs.

Throughout history neither individuals nor nations have been required to suffer attack before exercising the natural right of self-defense. But to prevent this right of self-defense from being employed falsely to justify unprovoked aggression or "preventive" wars, international norms have arisen requiring a threat to be *immediate* and *unavoidable* to justify preemptive action.

The evidence submitted by the United States and Great Britain to the world community concerning both the immediacy and unavoidability of Iraq's threat has, up to now, proved spectacularly deficient. But, to be generous, something may turn up. The issue is, where do we go from here? Will the doctrine of preemption become a centerpiece and enduring construct of U.S. national security policy? And, if so, who is next?

Answers may reside in the evolution of the doctrine of preemption under the second Bush administration during the period between the 9/11 attacks and the presentation of its national security strategy in February 2003. On September 14, 2001, the president declared, "Our responsibility to history is already clear: to answer these attacks and to rid the world of evil."[3] Echoing Ronald Reagan's "evil empire" construct and anticipating his own "axis of evil," President Bush here introduces his theocratic foreign and defense vision.

According to the Bush national security strategy, the traditional definition of imminence used to justify preemption was the visible mobilization of traditional armies and navies in preparation for attack. Rogue states and terrorists, however, use weapons of mass destruction that are easily concealed, covertly delivered, and used without warning. Targets for such attacks include civilian populations in violation of the principal norms of the law of warfare. (Here fairness, however uncomfortable, requires the observation that many nations in modern times, including the United States, have purposely targeted civilian populations in violation of the laws of warfare.)

The United States, the national security strategy continues, has long maintained the preemptive option to counter a "sufficient threat" (here undefined). The greater this threat, the greater the need for "anticipatory action" even if the time and place of the attack are uncertain. The United States cannot "remain idle" while danger gathers. The purpose of preemptive attack will be to eliminate a specific threat, according to the security strategy.

Analysis is required. First, is the goal to "rid the world of evil" aimed at terrorist evil or all evil? Even if it means only terrorist evil, there is still an important distinction between terrorist evil aimed at the United States and terrorism—Chechnyan, Philippine, Palestinian—aimed at others. Is it merely the former, or is it both? And if the goal is riddance of all evil in the world, we are in for a busy, and possibly remarkably eventful, century. The moral confusion over targeting civilians has already been observed. Presuming President Bush means that targeting civilians to start a war, rather than seeking to end one, is impermissible, then he should say so.

Then we come to the ambiguous phrase "sufficient threat." As Iraq has already proved, sufficiency may lie in the eye of the beholder. What seemed, at least to the United States and the United Kingdom, but not to continental Europe and others, to be "sufficient" turned out to be not very sufficient at all if we mean a threat against us sufficient to require preemptive warfare. Likewise, "anticipatory action" is ambiguous, but presumably it is meant as a milder synonym for preemptive warfare.

The hollowness of the rhetorical option of remaining idle in the face of imminent terrorist or other attack is discussed elsewhere. For now suffice it to observe that no proponents of this straw-man option are anywhere to be found. Finally, the Bush preemptive doctrine will be exercised, according to the national security strategy, to eliminate specific threats. Since preemptive invasion was first undertaken in Iraq, it is legitimate to ask, What was the *specific* threat meant to be eliminated?

To some, particularly unquestioning supporters of preemptive invasion and occupation—namely, imperial behavior— this analytic consideration of the doctrine of preemption will seem overly scrupulous at best and petty at worst. But a much more rigorous version of this exercise is exactly what "the norms of the law of warfare" as well as other serious strategic thinking are all about.

Wise leaders, particularly those proposing new military strategies and pursuing visions of empire, make things simpler, not more confusing, to the world and to their own people.

Resentment and the New Security

Much of the world will resent and oppose us, if not for the simple fact of our preeminence, then for the fact that others often perceive the United States as exercising its power with arrogance and self-absorption," according to the report "New World Coming."[4] It does not go without notice in the world, especially the impoverished world, that the United States consumes a quarter of the world's energy and produces a quarter of the world's pollution and trash. We daily throw away what to hundreds of millions of people would be treasures. And to say that this will all be overlooked because multitudes of people would like to live in the United States is to miss the point; we are seen by many not only as rich but also as arrogant, arbitrary, and wholly self-interested. As a consequence, resentment of the conduct of the United States is widespread.

Here let us return to the four revolutions outlined at the outset—globalization, or the internationalization of finance, trade, and commerce; the information revolution that replaced replaced manufacturing as our economic base; the erosion of the authority and sovereignty of the nation-state, especially among artificially created states; and the transformation of war and the changing nature of conflict represented by the new age of terrorism. If globalization opens an even wider gap between haves and have-nots, it will increase poverty and despair, widen cultural clashes, and dramatically increase resentment against us. If the information revolution also adds a digital divide between the computer literate with future opportunities and the computer illiterate without those opportunities, it will swell the swamp of despair, the breeding pool of future terrorists, theocratic absolutists, and nihilistic revolutionaries. According to one analysis, "We should expect conflicts in which adversaries, because of cultural affinities different from our own, will resort to forms and levels of violence shocking to our sensibilities."[5]

This new age requires, at the very least, a new definition of security and, to achieve it, a toolbox filled with more than weapons. National security in the twenty-first century will require economic and diplomatic tools, not simply military ones. Trade and aid programs must become more grassroots and human scale than top-down and bureaucratic. For example, as mentioned earlier, microloan programs directed at home, land, and small business ownership have proved enormously promising in several countries in Asia and Latin America. The most often cited example of grassroots lending is the Grameen ("village" in Bangla) Bank, started in 1976, which specializes in microloans to individuals and villages. Over the past quarter century, the bank has made more than 83,000 loans to entrepreneurs, for village phones, and for scholarships to poor students. It is 90 percent owned by the 3 million rural poor whom it serves. Likewise, Hernando de Soto, author of *The Mystery of Capital,* has long advocated and lobbied for microloans to create property rights and ownership among the urban and rural poor of Peru.[6] In the political arena, our diplomacy must increasingly take into account expanding interests we have in common with people of goodwill around the world and be based on the principles underlying our Constitution and nation—principles of honor, of humanity, of respect for difference—and it must be aimed at people, not just governments. We can explain our principles and ideals much better than we have done, but we must then also be prepared to live up to them. The ideals of democracy are not marketed; they are lived.

Of the three resources required by terrorists—money, weapons, and people—the most vital one is people. Our "war on terrorism" should aim, where possible, to dry up the swamp of despair found in refugee camps, favelas, and impoverished villages throughout the world. As the writer Robert Kaplan has pointed out, for millions of young people who live in such conditions, barracks life and terrorist training camps are a step up. Though the first suicidal attackers did not come from refugee camps, it is a likely prospect that the next wave will.

A Reformed Military

The military component necessarily remains at the center of national security. Few doubt that legitimate requirements for the use of force in our defense will continue to arise despite our best efforts to replace misery and hopelessness with opportunity and democracy. But the military of the twenty-first century must look different and perform much differently from that of the twentieth. We will need at least five separate kinds of military capabilities: nuclear capabilities, decidedly smaller than during the Cold War, to deter enemies from strategic attack; homeland security capabilities; conventional capabilities sufficient to win major wars; rapidly deployable expeditionary and intervention capabilities; and humanitarian relief and constabulary capabilities.[7] Paradoxically, our military establishment will become more technological, but it will also be more dependent on human skill and performance. Technologically, our military will expand into space. But that component must be defensive, not offensive. It would be a mistake of immense proportion to encourage or even permit introduction of weapons into space, let alone take the lead in doing so.

United States military forces of the twenty-first century will look different, literally, but they will also be organized differently. Increasingly, brigade- and regiment-sized units will replace the traditional large divisions in importance. Their characteristics and values will be speed, precision, and intelligence. Why blow up everything when you can blow up one thing and still get the job done? The various services will conduct more joint and combined training, and their command, control, communications, computer, and intelligence systems will be more integrated across service boundaries. Greater importance will be given to anticipation of crises before they occur, and cooperative security arrangements will provide basing, equipment prepositioning, and overflight rights before, not after, conflict arises. Perhaps most important, special forces such as Delta, Rangers, and Seals will train and operate more jointly and eventually might even become a formal fifth service branch.

In terms of equipment, both the navy and the air force require more strategic lift, air, and sea transport to move troops and equipment rapidly and then resupply them. The army and marines require less heavy armor for traditional battlefield engagements and more light, quick, and flexible armor for urban warfare, and both can replace many helicopters vulnerable to shoulder-fired surface-to-air missiles with unmanned aircraft.

In addition to increased sea-lift, the navy must convert some ballistic missile submarines to cruise missile launchers. As fixed land bases become more difficult to maintain in the trouble spots where an American military presence may be legitimately required, greater weight and importance will be given to the offshore basing represented by carrier-led task forces. Mobility, flexibility, and sustainability will become even more important naval attributes over time. Large-scale, land-based, forward-deployed forces are in decline; small-scale forces are limited in capability, and therefore vulnerable, and are often maintained to demonstrate political support. Naval fleets can quickly depart, it is argued, but so can small onshore enclaves.

Further, the twenty-first-century military will also involve more precision-guided munitions. In the first Gulf War in

1991, 10 percent of munitions were precision guided, and even those were not as consistently accurate as we were led to believe. In the Afghan war in 2002, 90 percent of our munitions were precision guided. But that dramatic increase in precision guidance did not prevent us from bombing the wrong targets. Precision is an asset only if the human factor, accurate intelligence, controls.

We are indeed, as some have emphasized, in a "revolution of military affairs" largely driven by technology but dependent on intelligence collected and analyzed by humans. Our fighting forces are increasingly directed by and through a complex web of computerized information, command, control, and communications networks all interwoven and interrelated. The first Persian Gulf war was directed from a makeshift headquarters in Saudi Arabia. A decade later the Afghan war continues to be directed from Central Command in Florida. We are adopting unmanned air vehicles (UAVs) and unmanned combat air vehicles (UCAVs) as fast as we can produce them. The commander in chief in the White House now can monitor real-time pictures from these vehicles in the combat zone.

But high technology can be both extremely vulnerable to and dependent on the human actor. Exotic Pentagon communications networks are vulnerable to "twenty-one-year-old hackers." And precision-guided munitions on board B-52s flying from Diego Garcia or fighter-bombers launched from aircraft carriers in the Indian Ocean were guided by Delta Force personnel wearing civilian clothes and riding mules across the hills of Afghanistan. Despite our sophisticated targeting systems, a wedding party was wiped out because of the failure of human intelligence.

Paradoxically, once again, the most technologically superior superpower in human history is now dependent on human ingenuity more than ever. If intelligence fails, as it did with terrorist attacks on the World Trade Center and the Pentagon, all the technology in the world cannot save us. To know when, where, and how terrorists intend to strike, and what they intend to use to do so, is almost entirely dependent on human intelligence collection. Electronic surveillance methods, overhead intelligence satellites, telecom intercepts and wiretaps, bugging and pursuing all together cannot replace the human agent.

In the age of terrorism and "crime-war," we will continue to need expeditionary forces when major conflicts arise. But these must be lighter and swifter than the heavily armored, often cumbersome ground forces of the past. Getting to the conflict fast is now often more important than getting there in massive size. Ultrasophisticated, post–Cold War conventional weapons platforms—ships, planes, and tanks—will have to be different. Despite our enormous wealth, we can no longer afford to integrate technology so closely to platforms that the platform must be replaced when technology changes—as it does with lightning speed. We cannot afford ships, planes, and tanks that are outdated the year they come into service, if not before. Platforms—once again, ships, planes, and tanks—must be built for durability and long life. The weapons and sensors we place on them must be "plugged in," that is, readily removable when new technologies become available.

Two illustrations are the venerable B-52 bomber and the aircraft carrier. The B-52, now in its sixth decade of life, is still performing—even though it is older than the *fathers* of the pilots who fly it. We also keep aircraft carriers in service for more than half a century. These platforms rarely change. But the technological sensors and weapons change almost overnight these days. Even so, human ingenuity will continue to trump technology. Delta Force, as mentioned, used a 3,000-

year-old transportation system, the mule, to direct twenty-first-century technology.

The roots of the Defense Department's belated and uneven attempts to make the transition from twentieth-century weapons and warfare to preparation for what some have called the "fourth generation of warfare" of the twenty-first century trace to the military reform movement of the late 1970s. Even then, reformers were advocating unit cohesion and officer initiative, maneuver doctrine and tactics, and lighter, faster, more replicable weapons. Without attention to new people policies and innovative strategy, tactics, and doctrine, cancellation of weapons such as the Crusader artillery piece will by themselves not transform the military sufficiently for a new kind of conflict.

Military Power and Popular Sovereignty

The support of the American people is crucial to any military undertaking, and the longer a military engagement may take, the more crucial popular support becomes. Consequently, the people must know, as accurately as possible, the estimated costs of our commitments. They must know which significant members of the international community openly support us, including those who will provide military resources. Most of all, they must be given the most candid casualty estimates available for both sides. We were told none of these things when we invaded Iraq. It cost us 58,000 American lives in Vietnam to learn the lesson that the American people must not be misled, lied to, or treated as unable to understand the costs and duration of military engagements.

Any grand strategy, and its subset, a national security strategy, must recognize that the United States military does not belong to the president; under our Constitution the military belongs to the American people, who elect a president to command it. Public support for commitment of our military to combat is crucial for its success. That support cannot be granted in the dark and without a candid statement by the commander in chief regarding the probable costs in human lives and national treasure.

Sound strategy requires that military engagements be undertaken only after the nation is prepared for their consequences. Such was not done in the war on Iraq. The United States was not prepared for what the secretary of defense, among others, believed would be virtually inevitable retaliatory terrorist attacks on the United States for our invasion of an Islamic country. A Council on Foreign Relations task force reported that we were woefully unprepared for, and are still at risk from, future terrorist attacks: "A year after September 11, 2001, America remains dangerously unprepared to prevent and respond to a catastrophic terrorist attack on U.S. soil."[8] It is imprudent in the extreme preemptively to attack a nation in a region seething with hostile suicidal forces when we are still vulnerable to their retaliation.

From this discussion, the outlines of a national security structure and a set of strategies, tactics, and doctrines necessary to protect us in an age of multiple revolutions can be drawn. We must understand the changing nature of conflict and the concurrently changing nature of security. We must appreciate the nature of threats and respond to the causes of those threats not only with military means but also with economic and diplomatic imagination to reduce the despair that fuels terrorism. The military means we use when necessary will look dramatically different from those of the recent Cold War age. Our military assets should capitalize on our technological superiority but recognize its increasing dependence on skillful human direction. And homeland security must achieve a balance between security and liberty by constant recognition of our peculiar constitutional heritage and the mandate that heritage provides to rely on citizens and citizen-soldiers devoted to civic virtue and civic duty.

7 ✳

Who We Are

Temptations of Empire

The United States will sacrifice its character as a republic if it aspires to the role of empire, even a benign and liberal empire. "It is a rare moment and special opportunity in history when the acknowledged dominant global power seeks neither territory nor political empire," observed one group of Americans (perhaps too hastily).[1] For several reasons this issue is central to America's character: the resources required to maintain the empire, the political transformation required in the United States, and the change in cultural values an empire requires.

As wealthy as America is, and by any historical standard it is wealthy indeed, it does not possess, nor can it produce, sufficient wealth to provide for the security of its citizens, offer opportunity to future generations of middle-class and lower-income people, pay for future health care and retirement programs, maintain occupying armies and civil administrations in the Middle East and other troubled regions of presumed interest, invest in technological research and innovation, and balance its budgets. The British Empire finally collapsed in the 1950s because it bankrupted itself and the United States was unwilling to lend it money and pay the costs of maintaining its extended sovereignty.

Politically, even the most ardent advocates of U.S. imperialism have yet to define where we should and should not impose our will and our cultural values. Though they will not openly and honestly say so, the larger Middle East, to include much of the Arab world, seems to be a principal imperial target and goal. Exactly what our long-term purposes are—whether the economic importance of oil reserves or the political importance of settling Israel and Palestine—we have yet to be candidly told. The myth of suppressing terrorism will hold only until our prolonged military occupation of parts of the region provokes the terrorist attacks on America that it surely will.

The question repeatedly recurs: How far does our empire go, and where does it all end? Suppose, for example, trouble in Mexico produces increased floods of illegal immigrants and refugees into California and Texas, border friction, and clashes between radical, renegade Mexican factions and the U.S. Border Patrol. Suppose, further, this upheaval threatens Mexican oil exports to the United States. There certainly would be U.S. "interests" in suppressing violence, reducing immigration, and restarting oil flows. In terms of oil supplies (there it is again), the same would be true of Venezuela. But what of other Latin nations? Would the United States display its benign imperial reach to deter a wave of repressive authoritarian governments in Argentina, Brazil, or Chile?

Then there is Africa to consider. Surely a radical fundamentalist regime in Cairo would threaten our designs in the Middle East. The Mubarak government, which we pay handsomely to behave and maintain internal order, will not last forever. Post-Qaddafi Libya, whose oil will shortly reenter world markets, could migrate in any number of directions. Then there are the expanding oil reserves being discovered in

West Africa. How shall the new American empire go about establishing and maintain benign and friendly governments in half a dozen or so countries to guarantee the availability of that oil? Once massive investments by American oil companies are made in production and transmission facilities in West Africa, Rwanda-style tribal slaughter threatening those investments cannot be tolerated.

Across in Asia a fundamentalist takeover in a major nation such as Indonesia, with a population of 800 million people, would threaten the peace and stability of a wide region, not to say also strategic maritime choke points such as the Strait of Molocca. And in the Indian subcontinent, the fate of Pakistan, less stable and secure than we suppose it to be, invites American imperial interest. A Pakistan in the hands of a burgeoning new bin Laden, with nuclear weapons at his disposal, would be sorely tempted to rally nationalist and fundamentalist religious fervor behind reclaiming Kashmir and Jammu and settling long-standing scores with secular India. The American empire could not afford to let this happen.

All this and more, without mentioning the troublesome future of Saudi Arabia, semivisible cankers such as Taiwan and China, the technical state of war between Russia and Japan over the Kyril Islands (or Northern Territories), make the world an interesting and challenging place for a putative American empire.

It is not enough to say the United States will exercise its benign and liberal influence where it has "interests." It has interests in all these places, and more. In most, if not all, of these significant places of interest and importance, politics is complex, economies are troubled, and ethnic and cultural currents are layered. The exercise of American imperial influence would in almost all cases require at least some military intervention and occupation and long-term civil administration on a scale approximating our involvement in Iraq. If only two or three of these nations or regions required American supervision, the size of our armed forces and military presence and the costs of occupation and administration would be, as the Iraqi experience is proving, staggering.

As current federal deficits prove, these costs will be paid at the expense of education for our children, care for our elderly, and investment in innovation. They will also entail other political and social costs. Extended foreign military deployments, once again as illustrated by Afghanistan and Iraq, will deter reenlistments and choices toward military careers and, therefore, invite the alternative of conscription. How many young Americans are sufficiently interested in the American empire to interrupt their education, employment, and family life to serve it? Certainly careers will open up in a dramatically expanded diplomatic corps (Colonial Office?). But these will become less appealing as American colonial headquarters in Cameroon, Karachi, and Baghdad become walled enclaves and the natives take it upon themselves to sweeten the morning coffee with strychnine. This not even to mention those nasty car bombs at the embassy gates.

To fulfill the ambitions of empire will require changes in American political culture and, therefore, political leadership of sufficient dimension to explain why America's values and purposes must change. If transition from the war on terrorism to "regime change" in Baghdad was an invasion almost too far, what will be required to convince Americans that security from terrorists demands selective preemption, preventive wars, then long-term military occupations, then a far-flung permanent empire? It is almost comic to suggest, as some have done with a straight face, that America has been an empire since Daniel Boone crossed over into Appalachia. America must "come to terms with the fact," counsels Niall Ferguson, "that this republic, almost from its very inception, began to behave like another British Empire."[2] A curious observation perhaps available only to a non-American.

Considerable imagination is required to suppose an American president straightforwardly declaring either that we already are an empire and should admit it or that we have no choice but to become a new empire with all the responsibilities, obligations, duties, and costs implied. This dilemma is highlighted by the revealing remarks of an advocate of the American empire theory: "I don't actually advocate a declaration [that America is an empire]. It would greatly alarm American voters who continue to bask in the illusion that their country's vast overseas military commitments and economic engagements and regular military interventions are in some strange way the actions of a non-empire."[3]

Right about the alarm; wrong about the illusion. In none of its current military deployments, save Afghanistan and Iraq, and none of its economic engagements does the United States undertake civil administration, administration of justice, imposition of property codes, sanctioning of political structures, or structuring financial institutions. Indeed, in places like Somalia and Haiti we were criticized for leaving before these things were done. It is a far cry from stationing forces at the request of a host government to support indigenous armies to undertaking to run a country according to our will and our own design.

The fear of alarming the citizens of the United States is well-taken. To publicly promote an American colonial empire and advocate its expansion is not a path calculated to achieve political success and widespread public acceptance. This may or may not have been President Bush's objective in Iraq, but he certainly did not dare employ the rhetoric of empire. And this is the point. Is it really the purpose of the advocates of empire, presumed or proposed, to achieve this grand objective in secret, to spread America's military and political tentacles without telling the American people what they are up to?

Such a suggestion is breathtaking in its audacity. It is even more breathtaking in what it reveals about the attitude of the neo-imperialists toward the American people. "Contempt" is too mild a word, "disdain" even more so. The theme of shielding the American people from the truth about their own government's imperial activities and ambitions runs throughout the neo-imperialist literature. One writer advocates "supremacy by stealth," recognition that the United States already "possesses a global empire," which it must manage "in the shadows and behind closed doors."[4] The stealth required for this historic American departure is not for the rest of the world, which will surely feel the harsh effects of America's shadowy enterprise, but for the American people, lest they awake one day to ponder exactly when they lost the Republic they were taught to salute and over which they were, at least in theory, sovereign.

There is a world of difference between a historic power such as the United States using its power and influence to organize the world community to provide security, expand opportunity, and promote liberal democracy, on the one hand, and the United States using its military power to overthrow governments, impose its own colonial administrations, and occupy foreign countries for many years, on the other. In the former case the United States seeks to impose neither control nor will, organizes the resources of others, exercises benign influence, leads rather than dictates, and is motivated by the common good and common interest. It is governed by its own constitutional principles and remains true to its republican heritage. In the latter case the United States advances its own interests at the point of a spear, sometimes covertly and surreptitiously, it governs countries directly through proconsuls or colonial administrators or indirectly through handpicked puppet governments, it pays its costs where possible through the sale of local resources, and its long-term presence or occupation is required to solidify the order it seeks to impose.

In the latter case the problem of selectivity is a real one. It might be called the North Korea or Iran problem. If, as was argued by the administration regarding Iraq, preemptive invasion and occupation are required to eliminate threats to our security, then the same approach should be used in North Korea and Iran (among other problem spots), which represent equal or greater threats. Given this inconsistency, at least one of two things must be true. Either elimination of a threat was not the real reason for occupying Iraq, or we will exercise the option of empire only in those venues where it is relatively convenient and easy to do so. It is not impossible that both things are true.

By deduction, then (since, again, none of this is being debated in Congress or discussed openly and candidly with the American people), the putative American empire will have these characteristics: nations representing the color of threat that can be conquered relatively easily will be targeted; it is hoped friendly governments can be quickly imposed, but long-term occupation and administration remain an option; the presence of a valuable resource such as oil will be an important and perhaps determining factor; the opportunity to condition the behavior of other nations in the region in our favor will weigh heavily; if the use of military power is too costly, economic leverage may be employed or political pressure applied; finally, the less public discussion of this strategy in the United States, the better. The American people should not be involved, as they might become alarmed.

This last point is real, not ironic or argumentative. The reason that citizens and taxpayers would be alarmed if straightforwardly and honestly presented the strategy of empire is simple: it is not who we are. It is contrary to our principles and beliefs.

Largely unmoved by arguments from principle, strategists of empire employ obfuscation on the grounds the American people are confused by idealized self-deception regarding our true nature and impatient with protracted foreign struggles. Both are patently false perceptions. Americans are intuitively clear about their political culture and values. And, as demonstrated through five years of World War II and forty-five years of the Cold War, we can bear the long haul—but only if we are told the truth, and only if the truth conforms to our basic principles.

There is always the possibility that the American people, out of fear of terrorism, desire for cheap oil, or just sheer arrogance of power, are now prepared to become imperialists and colonialists. However, strategists of empire should not bank on this character transformation, particularly when the costs of empire come due. Larger armies and navies, more invasions, systematic loss of troops to hostile guerilla factions, higher taxes, larger deficits—all have distinctly sobering affects. Even more sobering will be the fundamental changes wrought within our own society: loss of any sense of idealism; erosion of national self-respect; anger at systematic deception by our government; alienation from the global community; loss of popular sovereignty and dedication to the common good; and sacrifice of any notion of nobility.

Empire and its costs are the prices we pay for security, say the strategists of empire. This argument might bear some plausibility if empire, in fact and indeed, produced security. One need look no further than the closest parallel, the British Empire in the twentieth century, however, to understand the security fallacy. Take the bloody dissolution of the Raj in India, for example, and the even bloodier partition that followed British withdrawal. This, even though British rule was brought down by passive nonviolence and civil disobedience. Regardless of their proclaimed benign purposes, empires have a way of dying hard. But perhaps American purveyors of empire have it in mind to leave that matter to future generations.

Take even more, for example, the British experience in the Middle East between 1917 and 1945. For every propped-up ruling "friend" there were a thousand resentful enemies in tribal cultures resistant to central control, particularly foreign central control. The British left no stable liberal democracies in the troubled wake of their departure. Even in the case of the one exception, Israel, the British crossed its borders with what were to them terrorists at their back and what were, for the Israelis, "forces of national liberation." The struggle left behind continues six decades later, left largely for the United States to resolve.

Little consolation or encouragement is to be found for the United States in the British imperial experience. In fact, the lessons should be cautionary and sobering. Yet here we are, entering the Middle East as an imperial power as the British did almost a century ago. What future naïve and earnest power will be left to pick up the pieces after America's departure years hence must be a matter for conjecture, and perhaps sober reflection.

In his national security strategy (published in February 2003), President George W. Bush gave as the alternative to the doctrines of preemption and military superiority, and implicitly long-term occupation, "to remain idle while danger gathers." If there are proponents of remaining idle, they are also remaining silent.

There are a variety of alternatives to a strategy of empire based on preemption and occupation. The one argued for here is the strategy founded on principle. Advocates of an American imperial strategy emphasize the good works that can be carried out by an occupying force and a quasi-colonial administration. Those same good works can be carried out where they are requested; they need not be imposed.

A substantially restructured and reorganized Department of State, as recommended by the U.S. Commission on National Security/21st Century, can propose to help any nation, however backward and left out, to establish the rule of law; an honest and uncorrupt civil administration; a system of recognized property rights, market economies, free elections, freedom of assembly, and a free press; and a civil society required to protect and promote these and other liberal democratic institutions. The goal is free and secure societies offering opportunities to their citizens. In few cases is military occupation or imperial governance required to achieve these objectives. Indeed, in most cases the use of force impedes the process by requiring indigenous peoples to accept our ways rather than persuading them it is in their interest to do so.

In a dynamic world, "remaining idle" is not an option, and few serious people advocate it. The issue is whether America's purposes are best achieved through empire and force or through principle and persuasion.

Lest this argument be too hastily dismissed as supremely idealistic, even the most peace-loving republic has legitimate security concerns that can only be addressed through military resources and capabilities. The American Republic has survival, critical, and significant security needs that often require an American military presence, almost always (at least up to now) welcomed by nations hosting land bases and seaport facilities. Rather than being imposed upon reluctant allies, virtually all of these facilities are made available as the result of arm's-length diplomatic negotiations and generous lease payments. All of which leads to the importance of America's naval capability (the centerpiece of a maritime strategy) in a world where the availability of permanent, fixed land bases becomes problematic and American land forces on foreign soil increasingly become targets—as in Beirut in 1983 and in Saudi Arabia in 1992—rather than stabilizing presences.

The fleet can be in port for a considerable time, and then it can be gone. If welcome, it can stay; if unwelcome, it can leave. It can anchor visibly offshore or remain at length over the horizon. Carrier-based aircraft can project power ashore as can sea-based cruise missiles. The fleet can move from ocean to ocean, from trouble spot to trouble spot. Resupplied at sea, it can remain at sea for half a year or even more. It can support combat operations, patrol vital straits and choke points, participate in alliance exercises, and even host international summits and negotiations.

Though the nineteenth-century British experience offers a model, particularly in that the United States is also an island nation (at least figuratively), it is a great leap from having a maritime strategy to guarantee one's own security to having an empire to occupy and exert power.

Once again, however, lax language usage confuses the discussion. "Like it or not, the power and reach of the United States have already turned it into an empire," according to two writers, citing America's unrivaled military, economic, and political powers. "Only the United States can deploy a truly blue-water navy across every ocean, with 12 mammoth aircraft carriers each housing a modern air armada larger than the entire air force of most countries."[5]

If the simple fact of *having* power, rather than the way in which power is used, constitutes empire, then debate on this subject is useless. In fact, however, the way in which the United States exercises its power has at least two enormous consequences, one cited by these same authors:

> As the Iraq war underscores, the United States' great power enables it to act alone and still achieve many of its goals swiftly and effectively. But over time such a unilateral exercise of power will breed more and more resentment abroad to the point that other states may decide to work together to obstruct the chosen American course. Then, the United States could stand alone, a great power frustrated in the pursuit of its most important goals.[6]

This has been exactly the difficulty the United States has faced in engaging the United Nations in Iraq's complex reconstruction. Even more important, to exercise the United States' great power in a unilateral, imperial manner will be to change who and what America is. We cannot behave imperially and retain our republican heritage.

All empires end badly, and each ends badly in its own way. Too many volumes have been written on the how and why of the demise of the Persian, Roman, Spanish, Ottoman, British, and other empires to rehearse them here. Like nations, empires have individual characteristics that resist common description. Regardless of degrees of ambition, extension, reliance on force, and aggressiveness, however, most empires have shared common qualities.

Empires by definition are hegemonic. They extend their power and influence to nations and regions they dominate. They seek to have those subordinate territories follow their lead, submit to their influence, adopt at least some of their values, and mirror at least some of their cultures, all while surrendering at least some of their resources and treasures. To carry out their ambitions, more often than not empires are required to use force or the threat of force. Not all subjugation is benign or achieved willingly. Therefore, whether they originally seek to be or not, empires become militaristic. In the case of many empires their presence in alien cultures creates friction on their borders by challenging neighboring cultures and threatening further expansion. Then, eventually, the empire is drawn into such expansion in a restless search for its own unachievable security, and it becomes endlessly acquisitive. To administer and maintain an empire becomes increasingly challenging. Governance and regulation of far-flung territories require dispersed administration. But extension of political authority demands central control and, therefore, concentration of power in the empire's capital. Eventually, this concentration of power and the centralization of command and control, not to say the intricacies of complex foreign administration and suppression of dissent and resistance, lead to the corruption of the empire, not at its extremities but at its center.

Though these characteristics apply in varying degrees to the empires of history, they offer a guide to the character of empire even in the twenty-first century. But care must be taken. The nature of empire, or at least the condition to which the word "empire" is applied, is evolving and expanding. According to observers and analysts of the day, there are cultural empires (and subempires such as "media empires"), economic empires (and subempires such as "banking empires"), benign empires ("we wish no empire here"), reluctant empires ("we only responded to their call for help"), even inevitable empires ("there was no one else to restore order"). As with other instances of corruption of language, if everything becomes an "empire," then nothing is a genuine empire. In this confusion, it is important to preserve the central meaning of empire and the qualities an empire exhibits.

Empires have never been compatible with republics. A nation might originate as a republic and, as most notably with the Romans, end as an empire. There may even be instances of empires that eventually became republics, though none comes to mind. But there are no instances where a power, especially a great power, was simultaneously republic and empire. This is because their essential qualities are incompatible.

Republics throughout history have shared certain norms that are at direct variance with imperial ambition. These include commitment to civic virtue and citizen duty, the centrality of popular sovereignty, resistance to corruption, and a sense of the commonwealth. It is not simply that these values are directly contrary to the behavior and practices of empire just discussed. It is more that they are different in substance and purpose. Civic virtue does not relate to foreign acquisitiveness and subjugation. This is a large part of the reason the Roman republican army of citizen-soldiers turned into a professional, and largely mercenary, army when Rome became imperial in the first century B.C.[7] Popular sovereignty is incompatible with concentration of power and with militarism. The concentration of power required to govern an expanding empire is directly antithetical to any notion of the sovereignty of the people. Republican resistance to corruption is at war with the corrupting influences of empire. Indeed, throughout their history, ambition for empire has been a central cause of the corruption of republics. Commitment to the commonwealth of the republic is impossible to reconcile with the ambitions of hegemony. Consider, for example, the perpetual ambiguity of the status of Puerto Rico; "territories" and "possessions" have no real place in the American Republic's commonwealth.

In our effort to perfect democratic rights, Americans often neglect our nation's origins in republican thought and the duties those origins assume. Our founders spoke and wrote little of democracy. For some, such as Hamilton and Franklin, democracy was a plague and represented the threat of mob rule. Instead, being students of the classical Greeks and Romans, and widely read (in the original language) in Plato, Aristotle, Cicero, and Cato, among others, they created a republic. The constitutional debates, assuming republican parameters and language, focused on the *kind* of republic we should be. And that tradition became embedded in the fabric of our political culture. "I pledge allegiance to the flag of the United States of America and to the Republic for which it stands."[8] Suffice it to say, even regardless of the new realities of the early twenty-first century that make imperial ambitions problematic at the very least, America cannot assume the imperial role and remain a republic. The two are chalk and cheese, roses and raspberries.

These matters now require reconsideration because of the spreading assumption that the United States has no choice but to become an empire, albeit a benign one. Our status as the lone superpower, indeed "hyperpower," it is argued, as well as post–Cold War disintegration of old alliances, the failure of states, and the age of terrorism, all require us to assume the obligations of imperial power whether we especially want to or not. Among those advocating this position, the debate is not about whether but about what kind. We have become an empire, the argument goes; now we must define the nature of our new imperial duties and character. We are the largest economy, it is argued, and therefore we represent an economic empire. United States corporations have a presence in virtually all parts of the world. We are the dominant political power and, therefore, are a political empire. Our far-flung diplomatic and consular presence is unrivaled in human history. We have far and away the largest and most powerful military establishment and, therefore, are the default peacemaking empire. Not only do we retain at least token military presence in Japan and Germany well over a half century after the end of World War II, and in South Korea a half century after the end of Korean hostilities, we now have a very large military presence seeking to pacify Iraq and a smaller, but still active, combat force in Afghanistan. We are training counterinsurgency forces in the Philippines. Our fleet has a substantial presence in three major oceans. And we are a major peacekeeping presence in the former Yugoslavia. We are the de facto guarantors of the world's oil supplies, starting with Gulf War I. Most of all, we are the leader of a shifting multinational coalition conducting the war on terrorism.

Surely, taken all together, this is the profile of an empire if there ever was one. Contrary to neo-imperialist presumptions, the mere fact of having power is not sufficient, in and of itself, to create an empire; an empire arises from how that power is used. Now, much depends on the true intentions of the advocates of empire (and not all are forthrightly stated, even to the American people) and the length of time we maintain military forces to achieve our political purposes in a region. Our presence in Western Europe for a half century was generally (though not always unqualifiedly) accepted by host nations anxious not to be intimidated by the Soviet Union. Likewise, the Japanese, equally concerned about the growing power of the People's Republic of China and constitutionally reluctant to rearm, came, with some reluctance, to accept an American military force in the region.

The same conditions do not apply, however, to the new theater of conflict, the Arab and wider Islamic worlds. Efforts to create a semblance of democracy in Afghanistan are progressing more slowly than expected. There is now every indication that America's welcome in Iraq wore out long before our efforts at pacification, not to say at democratic stability, begin to succeed.

It is far from clear what America's long-run intentions are in the Middle East and the wider Arab world. Some policy makers have suggested that a permanent U.S. military presence in the region, initially established after Gulf War I and now greatly expanded, allegedly as part of the war on terrorism, is required to guarantee Israel's security and thus achieve peace in the Middle East. If that is indeed our objective, then we have become a hegemonic power in the region, and our military and political presence will be required for decades to come. We will not be welcome in all quarters, needless to say. Widespread resentment of American presence and culture guarantees that we will be engaged in low-intensity conflict, suffer attrition of forces, and find it necessary to carry out patrols and raids, thus further alienating indigenous peoples. If our extended occupation causes friction leading to conflict with other nations in the region, such as Syria and Iran, there will be a call to invade those nations.[9] The imperial characteristics of hegemony, acquisitiveness, and militarism will be institutionalized, and what may have originated as a vague effort to combat terrorism, having become long-term occupation, then morphs into classic empire.

How well do the characteristics of empire square with the large purposes proposed here? Let us review them. These are to achieve a new understanding of security beyond simply a defensive one; to expand economic opportunity at home and abroad by shaping the forces of globalization to offer security and opportunity for others; and to promote liberal democracy. Additionally we hope to base our international relations on common interests; to explore collaborative sovereignty in an effort to address common international causes; and to use our principles as a guide to our behavior. Let us consider how these purposes relate to the characteristics of empire.

Proponents of a "war-on-terrorism" empire have argued that U.S. military preemption of governments that may threaten us, if not now then eventually, enhances our security. But that is true only if the preemptive invasion and the "regime change" that follows reduce rather than stimulate terrorist retaliation. The war in Iraq shortly led to guerilla operations against U.S. and UN presences but did not immediately stimulate retaliation against the U.S. homeland. It is necessary to recall, however, that al Qaeda documents captured in Afghanistan substantiate the connection between the stationing of American troops in Saudi Arabia following Gulf War I in 1991 and the wave of terrorist attacks that began with the first attack on the World Trade Center two years later. It will take some time before we know whether initiating war against a major Arab state makes us safer or more in danger, more secure or less. Terrorists have proved to be patient.

The large purpose of expanding our understanding of security is to link economic, community, environmental, and other considerations to an appreciation of true security. Simply reducing the terrorist threat does not guarantee security in the proper twenty-first-century meaning of the word. And if the cost of a preemptive approach to the war on terrorism includes long foreign occupations and prolonged military deployments, nation-building, extensive governmental administration, and settling endless internal political disputes, all the while fighting off insurgent forces, all those costs are taken from the resources necessary to ensure genuine security at home. Additionally, the preemptive, imperial approach to the war on terrorism drains resources necessary for another large purpose, investment in American productivity that would empower us to expand opportunity and offer better alternatives to those in a world without hope.

With the exception of Great Britain, our major twentieth-century allies opposed our invasion of Iraq and largely frowned on a doctrine of preemption and preventive war as contrary to international law. They see our motives as much more imperial, and some of them have sufficient historical experience to know about empire firsthand. Thus, our use of the war on terrorism to broaden U.S. influence in any part of the world, but particularly one as fraught with peril and as rich in oil as the Middle East, is met with skepticism in Europe and elsewhere. By this approach not only is a century of alliance-building endangered and cooperation in the immediate war on terrorism squandered but also the possibility of establishing the common good as a guide for international relationships is greatly diminished. Since, at least in theory, Western nations in addition to ours are terrorist targets, it would seem obvious that conducting preemptive invasions as an antiterrorist measure, but one not seen as such by other threatened nations, might be counterproductive. The allies we will need in many ventures, including eliminating terrorism, should instead be appealed to on the grounds of common interest and common participation. A willingness to "go it alone" may be seen as a sign of strength by some in our government but will be seen by others, including important allies, as hunger for empire.

A new understanding of sovereignty requires examination of those new international challenges that can better be solved through new international institutions. Counterterrorism, peacemaking, nation-building, coercive weapons inspections, and elimination of weapons proliferation all will require less individual national action and much more multinational, cooperative action. This is where new approaches to collaborative sovereignty will be necessary. Preemptive U.S. action will make the collaborative approach virtually impossible.

Most important, the preemptive actions of empire—absent immediate and unavoidable threats of violence—are incompatible with American principles. Few believe that a previous American experiment with empire, the Spanish-American War, in which we acquired control over the Philippines, Puerto Rico, and briefly Cuba, ended well. Nor did it enhance America's stature as a democratic republic to be respected and followed. If the United States seeks to make much of the Arab world a new empire, even a benign one, it will end in even worse ways.

The Cold War required alliances in Europe (such as NATO) and in Asia (such as the Association of Southeast Asian Nations). There was little thought of going it alone against the threats represented by the Soviet Union and Communist China. Great diplomatic effort went into the care and maintenance of our alliance. Considerable economic assistance was offered to those willing to stand with us and join in a common defense. These political and military alliances with sovereign nations were the best, indeed the only, alternative either to the formation of an American military empire or to the isolation of the United States within its island fortress.

Almost exactly a decade passed between the collapse of the Soviet Union in August 1991 and the terrorist attack on September 11, 2001. During that period the United States produced no coherent strategy with which to address a rapidly changing world. With the 2001 attack, however, this strategic vacuum was filled by the "war on terrorism" as representing the United States' principal purpose in the world. We gained great sympathy in the world, including from former foes, and sweeping support in our efforts to destroy terrorist networks, including in Afghanistan. This international consensus collapsed, however, with the U.S. invasion of Iraq. We failed to convince the world that this war was a central aspect of the war on terrorism to which many nations had previously subscribed. The proof required for preemptive war is that a threat is "immediate and unavoidable." That proof was extravagantly clear in Afghanistan, but it could not be reproduced in Iraq.

Instead, in the brief interim between war in Afghanistan and war in Iraq, a new doctrine was introduced, the "axis of evil." In earlier days German fascism and Japanese imperialism came to be seen, though not immediately, as evil. Ronald Reagan famously called the Soviet Union an "evil empire." With these exceptions, by and large the United States had not based its foreign policy on theological assertions, preferring instead to accept the presence of wickedness and to deal with it by either containment or ostracization. The idea of a theological empire is a new idea in modern times, and it deserves to be analyzed.

According to the Bible, with Adam "came evil into the world." There is every evidence that it has been here ever since. There is no evidence that it will disappear soon. Assuming these realities, should the United States base its role in the twenty-first-century world on elimination of evil? This seems to be our policy toward Iraq. But, so far at least, containment, not elimination, of evil seems to suffice in other "axis of evil" states—Iran and North Korea. It is also not clear what constitutes sufficient evil in a nation to justify preemptive invasion. Possession of weapons of mass destruction, the threat of the use or sale of such weapons, and the threat of expansion seem to constitute qualification for the "evil" designation. In the case of Saddam Hussein, mistreatment of his people was an added justification for "regime change."

This is complicated stuff in that a number of nations, such as India and Pakistan, possess weapons of mass destruction. It is estimated that as many as twenty nations will produce biological weapons agents in the next decade or sooner, in addition to the dozen or so now possessing them. There is great fear that the Russian arsenals of biological, chemical, and nuclear weapons will be open to international markets, black, white, or gray, at any time if they are not so already. Reprocessing systems render otherwise peaceful nuclear energy programs into bomb factories. And then there are as many as forty or more dictatorships throughout the world that mistreat their people.

The notion of the United States becoming a righteous empire whose mission is at least to contain and selectively to eliminate evil is a novel one. At the very least a definition of those characteristics of evil requiring containment and those requiring elimination should be provided and debated. The costs of the exercise of righteousness in each case must be stated. Where inconsistencies occur, such as between Iraq and North Korea, they must be plausibly justified. Otherwise, American dispensation of righteousness will begin to look arbitrary at best and self-serving at worst. Why are Iraqi people worth saving, say, and not Tutsi tribesmen in Rwanda? Could it be the quantities of oil in one venue and not the other? If so, the moral foundation of the U.S. theological empire weakens considerably.

September 11, 2001, offered the first central organizing principle for foreign policy and military action since the demise of "containment of communism" and the collapse of the Soviet Union ten years earlier. Those whose ability to comprehend the world requires a villain seem to have devised this new mission for the United States—eradicating evil from the world, starting with Saddam Hussein. Having helped dispatch fascism in the mid-twentieth century, and later successfully facing off against expansionist communism, those requiring a messianic purpose for America's role in the world have found it in the "axis of evil"—Iran, Iraq, and North Korea—and more vividly in the personification of evil, Saddam Hussein.

The three "axis" regimes have little in common, and two of them, Iran and Iraq, waged a bloody, decade-long war against each other. Nevertheless, they combine somehow to replace the Reaganesque "evil empire" of the 1980s. One searches American constitutional history in vain for any justification for America's self-appointed role as the world's avenging angel. Thomas Jefferson, among others, believed there surely to be evil in the world, but rarely in the form of a political enemy. Patrick Henry would have come as close as anyone to casting George III in that light but generally avoided the temptation to do so. More often than not, American revolutionaries saw the monarch as a fuddled old fellow, an Enlightenment-age King Lear misled, on colonial matters at least, by his advisers.

Even for an American it is often difficult to parse the righteousness of the Right today. It is a matter for sober reflection whether the United States might have declared war on Hitler if he had confined the Holocaust within the borders of Germany and not transgressed against all Europe in the process. One will never know. But, in any case, there is a new strong impulse to have American foreign policy dictated by moral, if not moralistic, considerations. The principal question is, Where does it all end?

Having stagnated somewhere along Afghanistan's craggy border with Pakistan, the war on terrorism migrated to Baghdad. Had Saddam Hussein possessed weapons of mass destruction, the ability to deliver them, and the will to do so, there would have been a broad consensus among the American people—and our allies abroad—to undertake military operations to prevent him from carrying out his will. But some better showing must be made than has hitherto been done that those conditions were met. Though U.S. presidents find it inconvenient to remember this, the army still does belong to the people. And as bereaved and furious as the American people still are at the September 11 attacks on unarmed civilians, political leaders must still make the case for potential loss of American military personnel and local civilian casualties in wars to eradicate evil from the world.

But, presuming the case is made and the price paid, where indeed does it all end? If eradication of evil is the new foreign policy mantra, there are savage tribal leaders who hack off limbs, mendacious mullahs who stone alleged adulteresses, murderous mafia who gun down their opponents. If one is to believe the Book of Genesis, as we have seen, there will always be evil in the world. It is God's perpetual characterization of the human condition.

It is a minor irony that those in America who ridiculed Jimmy Carter's human rights beliefs as the basis for a "realistic" foreign policy have now trumped him by seeking to make America the world's avenging angel. One would not expect hardheaded foreign policy "realists" to be operating on good-and-evil wavelengths. During the Reagan and first Bush years (except for the "evil empire"), foreign policy discussions had to do with pursuing America's "interests." Now we would become the self-appointed scourge of all evildoers in the world. Our interest has suddenly become righteousness itself. It is as if the great abolitionist, mad John Brown himself, had become secretary of state.

Americans have largely forgotten that we ceased our humanitarian efforts in Somalia when eighteen American troops were lost. And we have truly forgotten the impact on American politics of seeing on television the large loss of civilian, and American military, lives in Vietnam.

President Bush did warn us in 2003 that the war on terrorism would not be easy and would not be over soon. Still, he did not say that our ultimate enemy was neither a ruthless dictator, nor a crazed rich fundamentalist, nor some left-over communists, but *evil itself.* Had he done so, then a debate might have arisen over whether adoption of a messianic foreign policy was exactly what we ought to be doing in this new millennium.

Missing in all this is any apparent awareness on the part of U.S. policy makers of the revolutions transforming our age and producing the kind of confusion that might cause righteousness to become America's default foreign policy. Globalization, the information revolution, the eroding sovereignty of the nation-state, and the transformation of conflict, as argued here, are all new realities requiring democracy's attention and response. If the United States neglects the historic importance of these revolutions, policy will be skewed. Even worse, it will be irrelevant. Righteousness is apparently meant to fill a vacuum created by America's inability to grasp the significance of these revolutions and turn them into powerful engines for global progress and the achievement of America's large strategic purposes.

Terrorists must be pursued down any dark alleys in which they choose to hide. But if that mandate becomes America's sole preoccupation and monolithic cause, we risk becoming a monomaniacal Ahab or a dreamy Quixote while the twenty-first-century world passes us by. Like Wellington reviewing his troops before Waterloo, we do not know whether a millenarian America as avenging angel frightens the enemy. But it certainly ought to frighten us.

The war on terrorism does not justify an American empire, not even one based on a crusade against evil. To pursue a theological empire would require a Department of State populated by priests, rabbis, and theologians, and to do so would surely threaten America as a republic.

State-sponsored terrorism is an act of war and, presuming proof, must be dealt with as such. The most effective way of dealing with non-state-sponsored terrorism is through the kind of international intelligence and law enforcement networks that proved so effective against al Qaeda after September 11, 2001. Such networks and cooperation preclude the necessity of invasion of states and overthrow of regimes but do permit coercive and intrusive inspections authorized by international authority. In other words, existing international alliances and systems are sufficiently adept at tracking and apprehending nonstate actors to alleviate the requirement that, absent an immediate and unavoidable threat, the United States act alone to protect itself. The alliance approach also assures that nation-building obligations and costs will be shared among a variety of nations and not assumed solely by the United States, as now appears to be the very expensive case in American-occupied Iraq.

The large purposes proposed in this book are incompatible with the United States as empire. They are based on the premise that America is the world's leader, that its leadership must be exercised in a revolutionary world, that its principles are one of its most important resources and powers, and that it will and must remain a democratic republic within the context of those principles.

8 ✳

Restoring the Republic . . .
and Its Principles

America as a republic, and a principled one at that, is central to our grand strategy and to the arguments presented in this essay. America's founders were united in the cause of creating a new republic. They debated fiercely what kind of republic it should be.

Throughout much of our history Americans have seen our country as a land of constitutional rights and economic opportunities. In the eighteenth century we fought a war for independence and liberty. In the nineteenth century we occupied the West and industrialized the nation. In the twentieth century we achieved material prosperity, at least for the middle and upper classes, and dismantled many gender and racial barriers. The cultural emphasis throughout this history was on the rugged individualism of the cowboy or the autonomy and independence of the entrepreneur. More often than not the national government was seen as the protector of powerful interests and the status quo by those left behind or as a barrier to individual initiative by those resistant to regulation.

We have accepted the necessity of collective action only reluctantly and usually in time of crisis—to save the Union, to survive a depression, to defend democracy against fascism and communism, to defeat terrorism. But by and large the American citizen's relationship to government has been a wary one, often skeptical and, in times of public corruption, even cynical.

Conservatives traditionally have seen government as the protector of vested interests, rights, and property and otherwise as a hindrance or as "the problem." Liberals have viewed the national government from time to time as the instrument of social progress but also, depending on its management, as a danger to their civil liberties.

None of this is necessarily bad, except that it obscures the other side of the American political coin. We are not just a democracy of rights; we are principally a republic of duties. Further, our nature as a republic presupposes a common good, a commonwealth, a definable national interest greater than a mere collection of narrow or special interests.

We have an interest in our common security, all would agree. We own immense wealth in common in our public lands, timber, minerals, and other resources, though ideologues and interest groups continue to press for their wholesale privatization (and perhaps logically so because the less we hold in common, the less the need for a national government to administer and protect common goods). We have a common interest in the health of our environment, though the extent of allowable pollution continues to be debated. And to some degree the rise and fall of our economy affects us all, except perhaps those with the gilded yachts and mansions on the hill.

Occasionally, national leaders—a Lincoln, a Theodore Roosevelt, a Franklin Roosevelt, a John Kennedy, and even, briefly after 9/11, a George W. Bush—challenge us to consider our common good and common interests. But when crisis recedes, we tend to return to our individualistic ways and resist the notion of collective action and responsibility. It is not uncommon, though, for those who have served in combat, or the Peace Corps, or in emergency response to catastrophe to recollect those experiences as the most intensely felt times of their lives and often the most meaningful and satisfying. We celebrate "the greatest generation" not for what its members did individually but for what they achieved collectively.

There is within almost every American soul a desire to make a contribution to some kind of greater good, to invest time and energy to make our nation better, to know the unique satisfaction of helping one's country and society. We call that sense idealism—the notion that the gap between what is and what ought to be can be narrowed if we will simply dedicate at least a portion of ourselves to that effort and that dream.

The world does divide itself between realists and idealists, or perhaps it is a division between those who accept a kind of Darwinian determinism dictated by fate or natural selection—a Calvinistic predestinarianism dividing the saved from the damned—and those who believe that nothing is "written," that the human condition can be improved, that none need be left behind. Robert Kennedy was noted for saying, "Some men see things as they are and say why; I dream of things that never were and say why not."

The sense of idealism has roots in political theory and reality. It is the very essence of the republic. From ancient Greece and early Rome, the ideal of the republic was founded on civic virtue—the sense of citizen duty; on popular sovereignty—the notion that we are self-governing and thus determine our own destiny; on resistance to corruption—requiring the common good to prevail over special interests; and on the commonwealth itself—the collective stewardship of all those things we hold in common.

The restoration of the American Republic is central to America's role in the world, but a republican restoration is also necessary if we are to secure our future. And that restoration is the best and perhaps only alternative to the temptations of empire.

The qualities of the Republic are related to each other and to the realities of our age. A spirit of citizen duty and participation is required to guarantee the sovereignty of the people. When citizens abdicate their duties, they are no longer sovereign. Popular sovereignty is necessary to resist corruption. For the classical republicans as well as for America's republican founders, corruption was not simple bribery; it was placing personal interest or a special interest above the common good or commonwealth. For having common interests was what gave the Republic meaning and purpose. Without a common purpose there was no republic.

Duty, sovereignty, integrity, and the common good: these are the hallmarks of the Republic. To secure our future and to pursue our grand strategy, we must restore these qualities to America.

In the twenty-first century, restoration of the values of the republic will be at least as important as the reiteration of the rights of the democracy in addressing our revolutionary age. For example, civic virtue, the duty of citizens to participate in public life and self-governance, will be vital to invigorating the community, the most immediate forum of government, in an age where economic power is spiraling upward and therefore out of control and where citizens will increasingly feel the need to control their political destinies.

And through the revitalization of communities, citizens can not only perform their civic duties but also exercise their popular sovereignty. Our national and state governments are representative democracies. Our community governments, or "elementary republics" as Thomas Jefferson called them, are the venues in which citizens can directly and immediately participate in the governing of their own affairs. The citizen's vote is cast in the representative republics; his or her voice is heard in the local republic. Only in the community is popular sovereignty immediately exercised.

When popular sovereignty is exercised, corruption cannot take root. It would require a lobbyist army of immense proportions to influence the decisions of thousands of small community republics all across America. Placing narrow, personal, or special interests ahead of the national interest and the common good is not just a definition of corruption in classical terms; it is also, sadly, a description of American government in the early twenty-first century. By the classical definition of corruption, America is today a massively corrupt republic. Some political scientists assure us that, out of the clash of special interests, the national interest emerges. Republicans throughout history, including myself, refute that idea. The clash of special interests produces corrupt government and citizen cynicism and distrust. One need only look to the sad state of public confidence in government today to understand the point.

And when citizens are distrustful, do not exercise their sovereign rights, and do not perform their civic duties, they are not prepared to carry out their most important duty, that of defense of their communities. Loss of a sense of civic duty, popular sovereignty, and the common good turns people inward. They think of defending themselves, in the manner of modern-day "militia," not the greater community. The changing nature of conflict, the emergence of the real and present danger of terrorism visited on America, now requires, for the first time since 1812, a new front line of defense, the citizen-soldier. The "first responders" in the war on terrorism on the home front are the citizen, the fireman, the policeman, the emergency health provider. We are all "first responders."

Globalization, information, sovereignty, and conflict. These revolutions of the twenty-first century summon forth the ideals and values of the Republic. As important as asserting our rights may be, such assertions are no substitute for performance of our duties, participating in our community governance by way of asserting our popular sovereignty, resisting corruption by putting our national interest first, and becoming citizen-soldiers in defense of our families and communities.

Civic duty, popular sovereignty, resistance to corruption, and a sense of the common good, these are the values of the republic and the necessary response to the new realities of the twenty-first century. In the real world of governance, these national values must form the basis for policies. This book proposes a new vision of security in a new and different century and a framework of ideas for achieving that security. It makes the large purpose of achieving security the basis for our other large purposes of expanding opportunity and promoting liberal democracy.

Security must include not only protection from violence but also the security of our livelihood and, therefore, income, shelter, nutrition, and health care for our families. It must include the stability of our communities and, therefore, protection from terrorist attacks, as well as protection from the massive dislocation of a bankrupt or relocated major employer. It includes the security of a clean environment and, therefore, freedom from man-made poisons in our air, water, and land. And it must include the security of all our children's futures and, therefore, protection of future generations from disease, ignorance, pollution, and poverty.

This new security is central to our common good. Its foundation is an imaginative program for public investment in our people, our public structures, and our private productivity. It is inherent in a foreign policy based on America's highest and best principles. It includes a new defense policy that incorporates military reform ideas and fourth-generation warfare capabilities with an understanding of the changing nature of conflict.

America's twenty-first-century strategy must be based on a framework of ideas for economic security through productivity rather than unnecessary consumption, for international security through principled engagement in the world rather than unilateralism, and for national security through new approaches to defense. New economic security requires a strategy of long-term investment in our people, our laboratories, our schools and universities, our productivity, and our infrastructure. It requires energy security sufficient to prevent the loss of American lives fighting unnecessarily for foreign oil. It requires rewarding investment and taxing unnecessary consumption and thus requires a reversal of our current national values.

New international security requires a foreign policy based on principled engagement, internationalism based on historic American principles of liberal democracy, tolerance of diversity, respect for difference of culture and viewpoint, and acknowledgment of an expanding global common. Principled engagement depends on shared security duties and rejection of unilateralism. It depends on expanded trade based on international rules for worker and environmental protection. It fundamentally depends not on America's selling its values and ideals but on its *living* them.

Our new national strategy for securing our future depends on an understanding of the transformation of war and the changing nature of conflict. We must have superior intelligence, particularly human intelligence, to achieve that understanding, new special forces to disrupt terrorist networks, and light, swift, and lethal intervention forces to protect America's legitimate interests. We must form a multinational capability for stabilizing or rebuilding fragile states. This national strategy absolutely requires a much greater sense of urgency for homeland security. And our new national security strategy for the future certainly means being smarter and quicker than those who wish us ill.

All these things—economic growth and justice through investment and productivity, principled global engagement, and a new national security policy—are central to securing our future and applying our powers to the achievement of our large purposes, in other words, to producing and achieving a grand strategy for the United States in the twenty-first century.

Conclusion

The principles and large purposes proposed in this essay are meant to suggest a *framework* in which policy can be made. They are designed to encourage new strategic thinking about how we should act on the world stage. And they are meant as a caution against how we should not act. It is not only possible but necessary for America to think and act strategically in the current new century: *to transform our domestic economy from one of consumption to one of production and, through long-term investment, to recapitalize our education and technology base and achieve energy security; to use the forces of globalization and information to strengthen and expand existing democratic alliances and create new ones; to employ those alliances to destroy terrorist networks and establish new security structures; and, guided by our historic principles, to lead international coalitions in spreading economic opportunity and liberal democracy and in nation-building, counterproliferation, and environmental protection.*

In pursuing this strategy we should not emulate European realpolitik traditions and practices associated with European statesmen of old. We are not a people who see the world principally in terms of the exercise of power, though its exercise is necessary when required for security and stability. Nor should either American political party, or any ideology, presume to possess a monopoly on the exercise of American power.

We should not hide our policies from our own people or from the world at large. In the long run, and increasingly in the short run, there are few if any secrets. Our policies must withstand the therapy of sunlight. In almost every case, except the most important security secrets, if we are afraid to disclose our practices or intentions, it usually means we will be ashamed of them when they are ultimately exposed.

We should not behave differently toward others, including the most humble nations, than we would have them behave toward us. Our dealings must be not only transparent but also fair and just. This is true all the more so since we now stand constantly examined in the court of international opinion, and we do not have the excuse of combating communism to rationalize our misdeeds. Even our resistance to terrorism must not become a new excuse to shortcut our principles, bully our neighbors and allies, and act as the new empire builders.

In the closing decades of the Cold War we oscillated between a policy of "values" (human rights) and a policy of "interests" (power and its applications). We should not separate our values from our power or our power from our values. A truly great power exercises that power humanely, judiciously, and fairly to all. Power exercised for its own sake, or for the sake of a selfish or expedient interest, is ultimately self-defeating. As a successor to the central organizing principle of containment of communism, this framework for a national strategy is based on democratic principles and republican values—a strategy that is resolute but is also one the American people can be proud of.

Our duties as republicans and our freedoms as democrats are the source of our principles, both for ourselves and for other peoples in the world. We can achieve a new kind of security in a new century only by constant resort to these principles. And we can preserve our status as leaders only through a new grand strategy that recognizes that our small planet increasingly requires both enlightened and *principled* engagement in our common human interests.

Perhaps most important, all Americans must now become engaged in their nation's conduct in the world. Our foreign policy, our relations with the peoples of the world, is no longer the province of so-called experts. The forces of globalization, the spread of American commercial and cultural influence, the internationalization of the Internet, the immediacy of travel, the rise of a global environmental common all now require the engagement of the American people. We must not let our role in the world be dictated by ideologues with their special biases and agendas, by militarists who long for the clarity of Cold War confrontation, or by think-tank theorists who grind their academic axes.

As war is too important to be left to the generals, so, in the twenty-first century, is foreign policy too important to be left to specialized elites and interests. In this century, the veil separating the foreign policy priesthood from the people must be removed. We, the people, must insist that our nation's finest principles characterize our dealings with our global neighbors. In this new age, our policy toward the world must be the policy of the American people—a policy that reflects our belief in our freedom, a policy that shows our desire to be friends and helpful neighbors, a policy that makes us proud of our heritage when we meet our foreign neighbors abroad and when we greet them here at home, and most of all a policy that leaves a legacy to our children that makes them proud of us.

For the first time since 1812, our security has become a function of the community. America will prevail in this new age more because of the strength of its citizens than the power of its military arsenal. But our citizens must be engaged in this fight, to a much greater degree than they have been, by our political leadership.

The new century of paradox dictates that the world's greatest power must look not to its far-flung branches but to its roots—not to its elaborate materialistic systems of production and consumption but to its ideals and principles, not to its greed but to its honor. From 1949 until 1991, we lived under the threat of nuclear war and depended on a policy of containment and a doctrine of deterrence to protect us. That was the basis of our national security. Today those tasked with carrying out the military aspects of our strategy are our neighbors and fellow citizens, men and women with homes and families just like ours. Their vigilance and sacrifice cannot be taken for granted or we demean our rich heritage of democratic freedom guaranteed by the bloodshed of generations of Americans who have stood the lonely post far from home to assure our safety and security.

War is not an instrument of policy; it is a failure of policy. We cannot discuss the use of military power as an instrument of national policy without recognition that it is the lives of our sons and daughters that are most immediately at stake. We all must now earn our rights by performance of our duties. And our duty to our sons and daughters requires our policy makers to hold their lives in sacred trust. Only then will our national security be both just and strong, and only then can we be truly proud of who we are.

These ideas—an encompassing plan for productivity through savings and investment, especially investment in our children, accountable economic systems, goal-oriented budget priorities, energy security, community governance, and public legacies—are not economic policies in the traditional sense by any means. They are meant to stimulate a different way of thinking about our economic values in the context of a new understanding of security. In the twenty-first century security will mean much more than freedom from attack from other nations. It must include security from terrorist violence, security of livelihood, security of community, and security for our children and future generations.

This economic framework is not partisan but American. It is designed not to rehearse stale old quarrels between Right and Left but to stimulate a new way of thinking about our economic choices and priorities. This framework is based on a commonsense notion—if we get our national goals right, reasonable people, imaginative, creative Americans, will figure out the right way to achieve them.

Most Americans are tired of a host of special interests fighting it out for bigger pieces of a pie that is not growing—a fight carried out behind the closed doors of the White House and congressional offices by people who have given and received vast amounts of special interest campaign contributions. Instead, let us establish our national goals and priorities for the twenty-first century. Those priorities will guide our public choices and economic methods and will truly enable us to achieve security from violence, security of livelihood, security of community, and security for future generations.

These new policy approaches, creating a framework for restoration of the American Republic, would resonate with that founder who continues to provoke our consciousness, that peculiarly eighteenth-century man whose vision reaches into the twenty-first century, Thomas Jefferson.

Politics today is too much about careerism, special interest, campaign contributions and access—what *I* need, what *I* want, about *my* rights. But the ideal is about the common good, or what is best for all of us, as well as our children and future generations. Politics is, as Plato said, "an art whose business is a concern for souls." The ideal of America concerns a nation of people still searching for a nobler cause, for a better destiny. We are better than who we are today. And because we know this, we are frustrated by the gap between who we are and who we should be.

America still represents a promise, a promise that democratic people can learn to live together better, that we can rise above autonomy and selfishness, that we can create a "city on a hill." We must challenge ourselves to join in realizing that promise, in holding our nation and ourselves to a higher standard, to use the creativity of our minds to find new ways to realize the passion in our hearts—a passion for a just society, for a great society, and for the ideal of the American Republic.

Appendix ✳

The following memorandum was sent to President William J. Clinton by the author on November 5, 1993.

Memorandum to President William J. Clinton

Elements of a New Grand Strategy

SUMMARY. Our nation requires a new grand strategy. For a half-century our consensus strategy was to contain communism and presume that an ever-expanding market economy would pay the costs of containment and produce a middle-class living standard for most Americans. This strategy is no longer viable or relevant due to the failure of communist ideology, the disintegration of the nation-state, the emergence of powerful, competitive trading blocs, and the erosion of America's traditional economic base. A new grand strategy should incorporate the following elements:

- first, it should coalesce the nation around an agenda for social renewal founded upon transition to a knowledge-based economy;

- second, it should establish a Grand Coalition among North America, greater Europe, and democratic Asia to establish a trade-based global economy and to support democratic institutions in developing countries;
- third, it should fashion a new definition of national security around military reform and a new definition of international security around collective peace-keeping and new security arrangements.

GOALS. The first objective of strategy is to state clearly the nation's goals. These are: to devise a modern economic engine capable of increasing productivity and competitiveness and producing economic security; to insure open global markets and fair trade rules; to prevent North-South polarization and the spread of fundamentalism; to support laboratories of democracy; to distribute responsibility for global peacekeeping. . . .

. . . Economic transformation is the centerpiece of a grand strategy for the 21st century. Without new systems for wealth creation, America cannot offer hope to workers and those dependent on society; it cannot generate the resources needed to address root causes of social unrest; nor can it play its inherited role in maintaining global stability and the balance of powers. Happily, as the industrial era and manufacturing-based economy decline, an alternative engine in the form of knowledge/information/communications-related industries is rapidly emerging. . . . Strategic marshalling of reform policies in education, training, investment, taxation and trade will be required to insure successful transition to a knowledge-based economy.

Productive 21st century economies must also be trading economies. . . . A post-Cold War strategy must prevent the former East-West polarization from quickly becoming a North-South polarization featuring waves of northward-moving immigrants.

By vigorously and systematically supporting democracy in emerging nations transitioning from communism, future military conflicts can be substantially reduced. When local and regional conflicts arise, existing and potential security arrangements must produce collective peacekeeping forces committed to intervene according to pre-arranged rules of engagement and exit. American military, weapons production, and intelligence structures are now totally out of proportion to any realistic threats. They must be reformed in terms of size, cost, mission, and influence if any new national strategy has any hope of success.

STRATEGY IN AN HISTORIC CONTEXT. The 1990s represent not only the end of a century and a millennium but also the end of an era, the Cold War, and the end of an age, the industrial. There are even more historic forces at work—the erosion of the nation-state—which require a new grand strategy. Traditional distinctions between domestic and foreign concerns—not least in economic globalization—are causing the disintegration of national boundaries. Nation-states are fragmenting under the external pressures of waves of immigration from the South and internal pressures of tribalism and ethnic nationalism. . . .

. . . AMERICA'S STRATEGY IN THE WORLD. The greatest periods of stability in European history were those guaranteed by an alliance of powers. The United States must create a new Grand Coalition comprised of North America, greater Europe, and democratic Asia, a coalition premised upon common economic and political goals. This coalition should have as its main objectives:

- maintenance of order in its collective spheres of influence;
- expanded North-South cooperation to reduce mass migration;
- constriction of the spread of radical Islamic fundamentalism;
- guarantee of open and expanding common markets.

The Grand Coalition, incorporating NATO and other security arrangements, should quickly resolve where its common security interests begin and end, prepare to protect those interests, and serve notice to radical fundamentalists, local warlords, terrorists, and renegade tribes and factions that the disruption of international stability will be met with swift and decisive collective force.

The end of the Cold War also requires a redefinition of U.S. national security interests. With the collapse of global communism, this new definition must be more particular, precise, and narrow than "containment of communism." The U.S. and its allies have no collective enemy and few common threats. . . . This is the ideal occasion for the United States to reform its military institutions and to better train and equip them for new missions relating to hostage rescue, counter-terrorism, low intensity conflict, guerilla warfare, and stabilization of new democracies.

Thus the twin pillars of a new strategy for America's leadership mission in the world are, first, a Grand Coalition of democratic nations guaranteeing open markets, international order, and collective security; and, second, a reformed U.S. military equipped and prepared unilaterally to prosecute newly and more narrowly defined national security interests.

NATIONAL ASSETS AND LIABILITIES. The U.S. is positioned to lead the industrialized world into the information age.

We have superiority in telecommunications technology, data processing and transmission, computer hardware and software, cable television systems management, satellite communications, and so forth. All these capabilities are converging, driven by fiber optic cable and digital compression technologies. All together these capabilities represent to the U.S. economy of the 21st century what autos, steel, and coal did to our early 20th century economy. Together, these "knowledge" industries form the core of a new national economic strategy.

Overall the knowledge base in the U.S.—schools, universities, and research laboratories—is sound and more widely-accessible than any in the world. This base will be crucial as the source of "knowledge workers" for the new economy. Although superior in access, our educational and training systems are failing in quality. Excellence, discipline, merit, and classical education must become the hallmarks of our knowledge base if we are to continue to produce a quality work force for the new economy.

Additional national strengths include military superiority, a stable currency, attractiveness to foreign investment, and political stability. . . .

. . . RHETORIC OF REFORM. The rhetoric of a new strategy should encompass these themes: restoration, reformation, and renaissance.

A new restoration includes the recapture of civility—community, work, order—all of which are disappearing from our culture. The restoration of civility opens the way for a new reformation, the restructuring of our society's basic institutions—government, schools, workplace, and even home. The reformation of our institutions can then lead to the ultimate goal for America—a 21st century renaissance.

This can be a renaissance of individual freedom, collective security, and civic virtue, a renaissance of artistic and scientific creativity, a renaissance of shared cultural values and social community. The great challenge, the one with which America has wrestled for over two centuries, is to combine the values of the restoration—order and civility—with the values of enlightenment, liberalism, and renaissance—tolerance, creativity, and diversity.

CONCLUSION. A new American grand strategy must include an economy transformed by the engine of knowledge/information/communications that will provide new and better economic security for a better trained work force, a trade-oriented restructuring of global relations, and redefinition of national security based on democracy building, military reform, and common peacekeeping. . . .

. . . A new grand strategy will require uncommon leadership undistracted by immediate, tactical considerations and committed to the long-term goals of a powerful but benign nation always in pursuit of the democratic ideal. The themes of this strategy for the 21st century are restoration, reformation, and renaissance.

Gary Hart

Notes ✳

INTRODUCTION

1. Zbigniew Brzezinski, "New American Strategies for Security and Peace" (speech, Washington, D.C., October 28, 2003).
2. See chapter 1 for a brief description of strategy and the broader concept of grand strategy.

CHAPTER 1

1. U.S. Commission on National Security/21st Century, "New World Coming" (Washington, D.C., September 15, 1999), 8.
2. Colin Gray, *Modern Strategy* (New York: Oxford University Press, 1999), 17.
3. B. H. Liddell Hart, *Strategy*, 2nd ed. (New York: Meridian Books, 1991), 321.
4. Edward Mead Earle, *Makers of Modern Strategy: Military Thought from Machiavelli to Hitler* (Princeton, N.J.: Princeton University Press, 1943), viii.
5. Paul Kennedy, *Grand Strategies in War and Peace* (New Haven, Conn.: Yale University Press, 1991), 4–5.
6. Samuel Huntington, *The Clash of Civilizations and the Remaking of World Order* (New York: Simon & Schuster, 1996).
7. Available at: www.usinfo.state.gov/usa.

8. Total imports of petroleum reached 9 million barrels a day by the fall of 2003, and imports of all petroleum products reached 12 million barrels a day, roughly 50 percent of all petroleum consumption.

9. Felix G. Rohatyn, "An American Journey" (speech, Chicago, November 1, 2003).

10. Individual and household debt reached $8.4 trillion in 2003. For the source on private and household debt see: www.mwhodges.home.att.net/nat-debt, April 2003. See also "Nation's Debt Grew at Rapid Pace in 2003," *New York Times*, March 5, 2004.

11. "U.S. Trade Deficit Grew to $41.3 Billion in September," *New York Times*, November 13, 2003.

12. Rohatyn, "An American Journey."

13. The wry parody of the American attitude is: "What's *our* oil doing under *their* sand?"

14. See chapter 7.

15. U.S. Commission on National Security/21st Century, "Seeking a National Strategy" (Washington, D.C., April 15, 2000), 6.

CHAPTER 3

1. See chapter 7.

2. U.S. Commission on National Security/21st Century, "Seeking a National Strategy," 7.

3. Brzezinski, "New American Strategies for Security and Peace."

4. U.S. Commission on National Security/21st Century, "New World Coming," 8, emphasis added.

5. U.S. Commission on National Security/21st Century, "Seeking a National Strategy," 6.

6. U.S. Commission on National Security/21st Century, "New World Coming," 1.

7. Fareed Zakaria, *The Future of Freedom: Illiberal Democracy at Home and Abroad* (New York: Norton, 2003).

8. U.S. Commission on National Security/21st Century, "New World Coming," 5.

CHAPTER 4

1. U.S. Commission on National Security/21st Century, "Road Map for National Security" (Washington, D.C., March 15, 2001), xiv.

2. Task Force of the Council on Foreign Relations, "America— Still Unprepared, Still in Danger" (New York, October 25, 2002).

3. U.S. Commission on National Security/21st Century, "New World Coming."

4. This point echoes the same disclaimer and caveat stated in the preface.

5. U.S. Commission on National Security/21st Century, "Road Map for National Security," xiv.

6. Rohatyn, "An American Journey."

7. Amory B. Lovins and L. Hunter Lovins, "Energy Forever," *American Prospect*, February 11, 2002.

8. "Why America Is Running Out of Gas," *Time*, July 21, 2003.

9. Lovins and Lovins, "Energy Forever."

10. Ibid.

11. David Garman, assistant secretary of energy, October 2, 2001, quoted in ibid.

12. U.S. Commission on National Security/21st Century, "New World Coming," 5.

13. U.S. Commission on National Security/21st Century, "Seeking a National Strategy," 9.

CHAPTER 5

1. Michael Dobbs, "U.S. Had Key Role in Iraq Buildup," *Washington Post*, December 30, 2002.

2. U.S. Commission on National Security/21st Century, "Seeking a National Strategy," 13.

3. Ibid., 9–10.

4. Brzezinski, "New American Strategies for Security and Peace."

5. By late 2003, under considerable domestic pressure, that projection was replaced by a plan for substantial U.S. military withdrawal by mid-2004.

6. Liddell Hart, *Strategy*, 322.

7. Gary Hart, "Enlightened Engagement" (lectures, Georgetown University, July 1986).

CHAPTER 6

1. U.S. Commission on National Security/21st Century, "New World Coming," 6–7.

2. Task Force of the Council on Foreign Relations, "America— Still Unprepared, Still in Danger."

3. Speech at the Washington National Cathedral, September 14, 2001.

4. U.S. Commission on National Security/21st Century, "New World Coming," 8.

5. Ibid.

6. See Web sites for the Grameen Bank: www.grameen-info.org and for Hernando de Soto: www.policylibrary.com/desoto.

7. U.S. Commission on National Security/21st Century, "Seeking a National Strategy," 14.

8. Task Force of the Council on Foreign Relations, "America— Still Unprepared, Still in Danger."

CHAPTER 7

1. U.S. Commission on National Security/21st Century, "New World Coming," 2.

2. Niall Ferguson, interview at the Council on Foreign Relations, New York, April 2003.

3. Ibid.

4. Robert Kaplan, "Supremacy by Stealth: Ten Rules for Managing the World," *Atlantic Monthly*, July–August 2003.

5. Ivo Daalder and James Lindsay, "American Empire, Not 'If' but 'What Kind,'" *New York Times*, May 11, 2003.

6. Ibid.

7. Ronald Syme, *The Roman Revolution* (Oxford: Oxford University Press, 1954).

8. In other written forums I have explored the degree to which the United States is still a republic and what it might do to restore its lost republican qualities. See *The Patriot: An Exhortation to Liberate America from the Barbarians* (New York: Free Press, 1995); *The Minuteman: Restoring an Army of the People* (New York: Free Press, 1997); and *Restoration of the Republic: The Jeffersonian Ideal in 21st-Century America* (New York: Oxford University Press, 2002).

9. Secretary of Defense Donald Rumsfeld suggested as much on more than one occasion in the spring of 2003.

Index ✳

Gulf War I, 26–27, 29, 93–94, 119–20, 140, 141, 142
Gulf War II. *See* Iraq war

Haiti, 129
Hamilton, Alexander, 139
Hart, B. H. Liddell, 21, 99–100, 102
hazardous materials teams, 67, 71
health care, 74, 78, 86
hegemony, 11, 13, 42, 52, 91, 99, 136, 138, 141
Henry, Patrick, 147
Hitler, Adolf, 147
Holocaust, 147
homeland security, 19–20, 53–54, 66–71, 81, 111, 118, 123, 142, 155–58. *See also* U.S. Department of Homeland Security
home mortgage deduction, 73, 76
hope, 9, 53, 57–58, 90
hopelessness, 57, 104
human intelligence, 120–21
humanism, 36
humanitarian relief efforts, 118, 148
human rights, 31, 89, 148, 160
Huntington, Samuel, 23
Hussein, Saddam, 12, 94, 145–47
hyperpower, 30, 139
hypocrisy, 29–30, 45

idealism, 29, 44, 53, 153
ideals, American, 25, 31–32, 36–40, 43–44, 91, 117, 132
ideology, 33–34, 44, 51–52, 72, 82, 161
ignorance, 45, 156

immediate threat, 50, 113, 145
immigration, 23–24, 38, 58, 126, 167
imminent threat, 10, 50, 114–15
imperial power. *See* empire
India, 96–97, 127, 133, 145
individual rights, 37–38, 40
Indonesia, 127
information revolution, 6, 13–14, 17, 42, 60, 97, 116, 169
informed consent, 100–101, 122–23
infrastructure, 67, 70, 75, 79, 83, 157
intangible powers, 24
interests, national, 29, 40, 44–45, 52, 126–27, 148, 152, 155–56, 160
internationalism, 32, 49, 59, 105, 157
international judicial system, 41
international law, 10, 19, 31, 108, 143
international markets, 55, 57–58, 60
International Monetary Fund, 26, 58
international organizations, 61–62, 97–98, 103, 105, 143. *See also names of international organizations*
international relations, 40–45, 89–106, 141, 143
Internet, 60, 161
investment, 56, 63, 73–79, 128, 142, 157, 162. *See also* foreign investments
Iran, 93, 98, 131, 141, 145, 147
Iran-Iraq War, 93

empire vs., 13–14, 16, 31, 40, 42,
  48, 130–31, 136, 154
restoration of, 151–58
security and, 68, 79–80
Republican Guard (Iraq), 102
resentment, 7, 9, 11, 24, 57, 113,
  115–18, 141
revenue system, 56, 73, 77–78
revolution, age of, 5–7, 11, 14,
  17–35
Rohatyn, Felix, 28, 81
Rome, 48, 138, 139, 153
Roosevelt, Franklin, 152
Roosevelt, Theodore, 72, 152
rule of law, 31, 32, 37, 40, 41, 59, 134
Rumsfeld, Donald, 175n9
Russia, 26, 59, 76–77, 85, 96–97,
  100, 127, 146
Rwanda, 49, 109, 127, 146

Saudi Arabia, 70, 98, 101, 127, 135,
  142
savings, 56, 73, 77–78, 162
Seals, 119
seaports, 71
secret policy, 45, 99–100, 129–32,
  160
Secure America plan, 73, 75–76
Securities and Exchange Commission, 76
security, 15, 53–54
  empire and, 132, 141–42
  larger understanding of, 65–88,
    156–57, 162–63: commu-
    nity security, 79–81; energy
    security, 81–85; generational
    security, 85–88; homeland

security, 66–71; livelihood
  security, 71–79
military power and, 98–103,
  107–24
in revolutionary age, 18, 42,
  47–48
separation of church and state,
  31, 59
separation of powers, 31, 90
September 11 terrorist attacks, 5,
  13, 30, 53, 66, 110, 121, 146,
  148, 150
small-scale forces, 118–19
socialism, 33
social safety nets, 50, 56, 60, 71–72,
  80, 87, 128
Social Security, 77, 87
Somalia, 4, 49, 109, 129, 148
Soto, Hernando de, 117
South Korea, 140
sovereignty of the people. *See*
  popular sovereignty
sovereignty revolution, 13–14,
  18–19, 97–98, 105.
  See also nation-state
  sovereignty
Soviet Union, 4, 14, 30, 60, 112,
  140, 144–46
space, militarization of, 52
Spanish-American War, 30, 144
special forces, 119
standard of living, 7, 83, 105
standing military, 50, 67–68
"starving the beast," 72
Star Wars, 111
steel industry, 60
Stockman strategy, 72

weapons of mass destruction, 70, 94, 96, 110, 112, 114, 145–47

weapons platforms, 121

West Africa, 127

Wilson, Woodrow, 32

women, empowerment of, 104

workers' rights, 57–58, 80, 104, 157

World Bank, 26, 58

World Trade Center bombing (1993), 70, 142

World Trade Center terrorist attacks (2001). *See* September 11 terrorist attacks

World War I, 102

World War II, 132, 140, 147

Yemen, 93

Yugoslavia, 4, 101, 108, 140

Zakaria, Fareed, 59